THE
NUS
OVERSEAS COLLEGES
STORY

Grooming Start-up Founders
at Asia's Top University

By
CHEE YEOW MENG AND GRACE CHNG

PUBLISHED BY

World Scientific Publishing Co. Pte. Ltd.
5 Toh Tuck Link, Singapore 596224

USA OFFICE:
27 Warren Street, Suite 401-402, Hackensack, NJ 07601

UK OFFICE:
57 Shelton Street, Covent Garden, London WC2H 9HE

and

NUS Enterprise
21 Heng Mui Keng Terrance, Level 5
Singapore 119613

British Library Cataloguing-in-Publication Data
A catalogue record for this book is available from the
British Library.

THE NUS OVERSEAS COLLEGES STORY
Grooming Start-up Founders at Asia's Top University

ISBN: 978-981-126-732-1 (hardcover)
ISBN: 978-981-126-745-1 (paperback)
ISBN: 978-981-126-733-8 (ebook for institutions)
ISBN: 978-981-126-734-5 (ebook for individuals)

For any available supplementary material, please visit
https://www.worldscientific.com/
worldscibooks/10.1142/13170#t=suppl

WORLD SCIENTIFIC
PUBLISHING CO. PTE. LTD.:

Chua Hong Koon
Lai Ann
Nicole Ong

DESIGNED BY

Redbean De Pte Ltd

Printed in Singapore

At NUS Overseas Colleges (NOC), selected students will work at leading entrepreneurial hotspots across the globe including Beijing, Ho Chi Minh City, New York, Shanghai, Shenzhen, Silicon Valley, Singapore, Stockholm and Toronto. At the same time, they take classes at our renowned partner universities like Stanford University and Tsinghua University. Our programmes run between six and twelve months for first-hand insights into innovative start-ups, and experience the challenges faced by the founders which would be useful when they launch their next big idea. That is why the NOC programme is not just another internship. It is an experience of a lifetime. We are home to over 3,600 NOC alumni who have founded over 1,000 start-ups globally.

About the Authors

PROFESSOR CHEE YEOW MENG is Director of the NUS Overseas Colleges (NOC) programme, Vice Provost (Technology-Enhanced and Experiential Learning) at the National University of Singapore (NUS) and a Professor at the Department of Industrial Systems Engineering and Management. As Director, he spearheads the university's experiential entrepreneurship education programmes. Professor Chee was also Associate Vice President (Innovation and Enterprise) from 2019 to 2022.

Preceding his tenure at NUS, Professor Chee was Head of the Division of Mathematical Sciences (2008–2010), Chair of the School of Physical and Mathematical Sciences (2011–2017), and Interim Dean of the College of Science (2018–2019) at the Nanyang Technological University.

Prior to entering academia, Professor Chee held senior positions in public service, participated in national level committees, and represented Singapore in various international forums and councils.

Professor Chee also embarked on the entrepreneurship path as a co-founder of a spin-off company and went on to found several start-ups before returning to public service and eventually joining NUS. He continues to be actively involved in the start-up ecosystem.

Professor Chee is a Fellow and Council Member of the Institute of Combinatorics and its Applications, and a senior member of IEEE. His research interest lies in the interplay between combinatorics and computer science, especially coding theory, extremal set systems, and their applications.

He received the BMath, MMath, and PhD degrees in computer science from the University of Waterloo in 1988, 1989, and 1996, respectively.

GRACE CHNG is a well-respected and deeply sourced veteran tech writer with a ringside view of key global tech events. She also has in-depth knowledge of the influencers and entrepreneurs of Singapore's start-up ecosystem. Grace was the tech editor for Singapore's morning daily newspaper, *The Straits Times,* from 1993 to 2014, where she wrote and edited stories on technology development and issues in Singapore and the world.

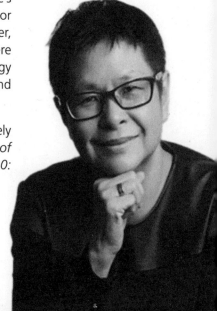

She has written two other books, namely *Intelligent Island, the Untold Story of Singapore's Tech Journey* and *Zero To 30: Singapore's Supercomputing Journey.*

CONTENTS

STAGE 3
THE NEXT 20 YEARS

INTRODUCTION

By Professor Chee Yeow Meng and Grace Chng

The acronym NOC is little known to most people. Yet the impact of this overseas internship programme of Singapore's oldest university has been profound. It was the spark that fired up the co-creators of two start-ups that have become household names in Singapore: Carousell and Shopee.

Carousell is valued at more than US$1 billion while Shopee is part of a US$8.5 billion e-commerce business of listed company Sea. They are some of Singapore's most valuable start-ups.

So, who is this low-key influencer? Born in 2001, it was conceived by the National University of Singapore (NUS) to engender a passion for entrepreneurship. The founders named it NUS Overseas Colleges, or NOC for short. As the name suggests, the initiative involves sending selected students abroad, where they will work for six months to a year in budding tech start-ups.

The move is strategic. NOC leaders believe that working up close with the founders will imbue undergraduates with invaluable lessons on what it takes to start and grow a tech start-up. Also, the location of these start-ups in tech hotspots such as Silicon Valley in California and Shanghai in China will inspire a dare-to-do mindset among the students.

They will earn academic credits, too. In each location, they are required to take entrepreneurship/innovation courses at leading partner universities. These include Stanford University in California, Tsinghua University in Beijing and the Royal Institute of Technology in Stockholm, Sweden. The esteemed names of these institutions were pivotal in winning over the programme's naysayers among parents and the faculty in NUS.

Now, 20 years after the inaugural batch of students left for Silicon Valley in 2002, the NOC's experiential model of education has captured attention. The Singapore University of Technology and Design has inked an agreement with NUS in which its students will be able to participate in the NOC programme from 2023.

Its achievements, in fact, were validated as early as 2010 when a panel of international experts on entrepreneurship education gave it a thumbs up after a review. It deserves on-going support, they said in an October 2010 report, and among the reasons cited is the boost it gives to the national innovation system.

The encouraging words opened the way for a second initiative that would further enhance the environment for budding entrepreneurs. It was launched in 2011 by NUS Enterprise, the entrepreneurial arm of the university that oversees NOC.

The vision was to provide a nurturing incubation space for fledgling start-ups. It became reality when a disused building in the Ayer Rajah industrial estate was spotted and retrofitted to offer low rents with support services. That building was Blk71.

In no time, it became a magnet for young technologists drawn by the opportunity to work cheek by jowl with like-minded techies and with dreams of creating the next big thing or becoming the Asian Bill Gates. The founders of online marketplace Carousell, online real estate agency 99.co and online discount shopping platform ShopBack are among the inspiring names that found their footing in the spartan offices of the seven-storey building. Soon, its name was adopted as the new scheme's snazzy moniker: BLOCK71.

Today, this concept of providing a focal point for start-ups to network and share their experiences has found wings and been replicated overseas in the United States (US), China, Indonesia and Vietnam.

The Dynamic Duo: NOC and BLOCK71

From the outset, both programmes were popular with NUS undergraduates. But their steady progress would, now and again, be threatened by existential problems. These episodes, however, did not distract the founders and top administrators of the schemes from the quest to take on an emerging challenge facing universities in the twilight years of the last century. That is, the increasing demand that they contribute to a 'Third Mission'. Entrepreneurship has become a new priority alongside the traditional missions of research and teaching.

This book chronicles the two-decade-long journey of this new mission, from the lens of the programmes' two key groups: their founders and the students who went on immersive stints abroad.

To round off the narrative, many NOC mentors, senior NUS officials and leading members of the Singapore start-up investment community were interviewed as well. In all, nearly 100 people were sought for their views and experiences.

For most of them, this is the first time they are recounting their trials and triumphs.

The initial trailblazers were a five-men team of NOC founders. They were led by Professor Shih Choon Fong, the then-new Vice-Chancellor and President of NUS and the late Professor Jacob Phang. Both men pushed and prodded for the creation of NOC. Ten years later, a team of three[1] followed in their footsteps and took the experiment to the next level in BLOCK71.

This book also sets forth the extraordinary opportunities arising from technology that spawned a new generation of entrepreneurs in Singapore. They came armed with university degrees. Their tales of tears and cheers are inspiring and hold invaluable lessons for any wannabe technopreneurs.

Among the fast movers are Jeffrey Tiong and Guan Dian. They co-founded PatSnap[2] in 2007. In 2021, it achieved unicorn status — a label given to privately held start-ups valued at more than US$1 billion.

Another duo, Henry Chan and Joel Leong, however, worked for a spell before plunging into the world of start-ups. They were employees for a few years at e-commerce start-up Zalora before teaming up in 2014 to start ShopBack, a cashback rewards programme for online shoppers on its platform.

One oft-mentioned name is serial entrepreneur Darius Cheung, who now leads 99.co, a fast-growing property portal that does business across Southeast Asia.

He plunged into the start-up world immediately after graduating from NUS and co-founded tenCube in 2005. The company developed a software that secured mobile phones, and five years later, it was sold for an undisclosed eight-figure sum to McAfee, an American computer security software giant. With his new fortune, Cheung subsequently co-launched a few more ventures start-ups before 99.co.

Soaring Figures of Success

The NOC–BLOCK71 double act is, undoubtedly, a striking figure of success when illustrated with statistics.

From the first NOC cohort of just 14 students in the US, the numbers swelled to 1,301 in seven locations by the end of the programme's first decade. Add another decade, and the corresponding numbers shot up to about 3,600 students at more than 15 locations.

These places are in entrepreneurial hubs across the world: in North America, there is Silicon Valley and New York in the US plus Toronto in Canada; in Europe, there is Munich in Germany, Paris in France and Stockholm in Sweden; Israel; in Asia, there is Shanghai, Beijing and Shenzhen in China and Nagoya in Japan; in Southeast Asia, there is Singapore, Bangkok in Thailand, Ho Chi Minh City in Vietnam, and Jakarta, Yogyakarta and Bandung in Indonesia.

More importantly, the pool of NOC alumni has created more than 1,000 start-ups, or an average of 50 a year. At least two of them are valued above US$1 billion: PatSnap and Carousell. Many of the founders have a rags-to-riches story and, **among them, more than a dozen have become multi-millionaires before the age of 40.**

NOC's contributions to Singapore were further validated by a 2019 survey[3] of its alumni. The poll shows they form a disproportionately large number of tech start-up entrepreneurs in Singapore. For instance, between 2013 and 2017, the programme had fewer than 1,000 participants, who made up a miniscule 0.5 per cent share of all graduates produced by all local institutes of higher learning. But they created more than four per cent of the tech-based start-ups operating in the country, and 4.7 percent of Singapore "scale-ups" with funding that exceeds US$10 million.

Further, the funding raised by NOC start-ups formed 3.2 per cent of the total raised by all Singapore-based start-ups, added the survey report. But if several foreigner-founded start-ups that raised massive amounts, such as e-commerce giant Lazada and multinational tech behemoth Grab, were excluded, the figure would jump to more than 10 per cent.

The figures also outline how NOC has significantly improved Singapore's tech landscape by broadening and deepening the national ecosystem for entrepreneurship as well as intrapreneurship.

"Besides the high proportion of alumni (one-third) who went on to start businesses, an even larger proportion had opted to work as employees in start-ups and other ecosystem-supporting organisations such as venture investment firms and incubators," said the survey report.

These intrapreneurs are highly sought after by established organisations, who are always looking for individuals with the drive, hunger and talent to innovate and develop new businesses.

The report also noted that NOC alumni are internationally mobile and able to thrive in an increasingly globalised and connected world.

They include Phang Min Chuan, the Economic Development Board's acting vice-president, planning and policy, Contact Singapore; Akash Nemani, who works as head of CPG, luxury and beauty products at Facebook for its Middle East, North Africa markets; Chris Feng, Group President of consumer internet company Sea; and Vanessa Tan, director of marketing, in Indonesia for Xiaomi, whose output includes consumer electronics and smartphones.

Singapore's Tech Pioneers

Singaporean digital luminaries and youthful tech multi-millionaires have, in recent years, burst into the public consciousness. The buzz had, at times, overwhelmed the fact that Singapore's digitalisation and computerisation efforts began as early as the 1980s.

Though public and private funds were scarce then, pioneers like Sim Wong Hoo of Creative Technology were undeterred. After graduating from Ngee Ann Polytechnic in electrical and electronics engineering, he opened a computer repair shop in Chinatown with a former schoolmate.

He was aged 26. The year was 1981, which coincides with IBM unveiling the personal computer that ushered in the personal computer era. In 1989, Sim had unveiled the Sound Card in Las Vegas at Comdex, the world's largest consumer electronics fair. It took the world by storm. In 1992, it became the first Singapore company to be listed on New York's Nasdaq.

Sim's early journey coincided with the rise of the Internet in the early 1980s, but like any new revolution, few could grasp its potential, let alone leverage on it.

Still, many executives in tech organisations who quit their jobs and became "businessmen" at a time when terms like technopreneur and start-up had yet to enter the common lexicon.

Among them was Wong Ngit Liong who founded Venture Manufacturing[4] in 1994 at age 53, after a thriving career at multinational information technology giant HP. Venture swiftly grew to be among Singapore's largest electronic contract manufacturing company in Singapore.

Another notable group came from two government agencies: National Computer Board[5] and Kent Ridge Digital Lab (KRDL)[6]. Many were youthful government scholarship holders such as Wong Toon King and Dr Lai Kok Fung.

Wong, who co-founded SilkRoute Ventures in 1994, one of Singapore's earliest internet company, is now a venture capitalist. Similarly, Dr Lai, from KRDL, co-founded BuzzCity to commercialise his research on a software that tracks updates to people's favourite websites. In 2016, it was sold to Mobads, a global advertising network, for a confidential sum.

Dare to Dream

Like the tech pioneers, the NOC alumni did not fear failure.

In our conversations with them, they credit it to their NOC experience, which they found "liberating". It freed them from conventional thinking, and in thinking out of the box, they improved their problem-solving skills and learnt to be independent, they said. They viewed failure as no more than a learning experience that would improve their chances of success in the next venture.

Over time, the NOC men and women displayed five traits not typically seen in their NUS peers. They were articulate, confident, critical, curious and driven. This figure of the bold and ingenious entrepreneur inevitably raises the age-old debate. What makes an entrepreneur: nature or nurture? The jury is still out.

Meanwhile, what is fact is that the NOC–BLOCK71 double act, in its first two decades, has produced a league of entrepreneurial-minded talents that has given a tremendous fillip to Singapore's start-up ecosystem. The start-ups they created and the venture capital firms they drew into the country have, in turn, bolstered national economic growth

But the double act is not done yet. This unique and innovative pursuit of NOC is, like the Singapore story, a never-ending quest. For now, NOC shows that immense opportunities await a person with a technological bent and who dares to dream.

THE
NOC
FOUNDERS

CHAPTER 1

OUR
Inspiration

Professor Jacob Phang was instrumental in setting up NOC which successfully nudged several NOC alumni to found companies such as Zopim and Peekspy.

With growing excitement, Professor Jacob Phang listened as Professor Shih Choon Fong, the new President of the National University of Singapore (NUS), laid out a bold change in direction for Singapore's oldest university on 1 June 2000.

"NUS will be to Singapore what Stanford is to Silicon Valley," Prof Shih declared in his inaugural address to the staff and faculty, as he outlined a vision that would see the institution put as much emphasis on entrepreneurship as it did on academic courses.

❝ We will aim to be the intellectual, entrepreneurial pulse of Singapore, the confluence of local and foreign talent. Yes, NUS will be a knowledge enterprise that transcends boundaries. ❞ [7]

The call to change resonated with Prof Phang, who was the rare academician with an entrepreneur mindset and a passion for putting research to work. He had founded SEMICAPS in 1988, a holding company set up to commercialise technologies developed at NUS' Centre for Integrated Circuit Failure Analysis and Reliability. SEMICAPS is one of the first, if not the first, spin-offs from the university's move to commercialise the research it developed.

After the address, the duo met to discuss how Prof Phang could help achieve the vision. They had worked together earlier when Prof Shih had been the Head of the Institute of Materials Research and Engineering (IMRE)[8] at NUS. Their discussion set in motion a long series of meetings that would give birth to a programme that has arguably become the most productive entrepreneur factory in Singapore: the NUS Overseas Colleges, or NOC.

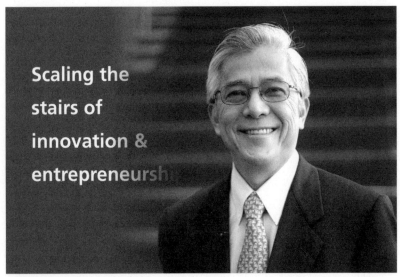

Scaling the
stairs of
innovation &
entrepreneursh

Professor Shih Choon Fong, who was NUS President from 2000 to 2008, envisioned NUS to become more like Stanford and to nurture entrepreneurs.

The Knowledge-Based Economy

In a way, some of the seeds of NOC were planted three years earlier when the Association of Southeast Asian Nations (ASEAN)[9] economies were trounced during the 1997 Asian Financial Crisis. The beating began with the collapse of the Thai baht, which triggered a chain reaction across the region. Most of Southeast Asia, including Singapore, saw their currencies slump, their stock markets and other assets devalued, and their private debt soar. The crisis heightened Singapore's awareness that it was no longer sufficient to be a cost-effective production base for business.

In February 1998, Dr Tony Tan,[10] the then-Deputy Prime Minister, said that as part of the push towards a knowledge-based economy, greater flexibility needed to be infused into Singapore's education system.[11] Students should be prepared for yet-to-be-invented jobs and yet-to-exist careers, he added.

As part of the effort, Dr Tan set up a committee to review the structure of the NUS student admission system. Prof Shih,[12] who was then the Deputy Vice-Chancellor of NUS, chaired this Committee for University Admission.

He had arrived in Singapore in 1997 after 30 years in the United States (US). The 52-year-old, Harvard-trained Singaporean was a highly-respected fracture mechanics expert and academician. He had worked in the US for A-list corporations like General Electric, a Massachusetts Institute of Technology (MIT) spin-off, and taught at Ivy League institutions, including Brown University.

He also regularly travelled to Silicon Valley, where the incessant talk was about innovation and research and development (R&D). Stanford University was also located there[13]. Combined, his working and teaching experiences, and travels helped form his new vision for NUS.

To become more like Stanford, Prof Shih envisioned NUS doing away with the bureaucratic mindset and nurturing the entrepreneurial spirit. It would ignite the spark for learning and encourage a free flow of ideas between staff and students, as well as across departments, faculties and even countries.

Most of all, he saw a need to nurture students who had gumption, enthusiasm and the daring-do to plant themselves to where the action is in the 2000s — Silicon Valley. NUS students needed an opportunity to feel and smell the place and to take the measure of their fellow peers. They needed to be immersed in the excitement of entrepreneurship, and in the discipline of performance. He believed the effect would be transformative.

Holding the BHAG

Prof Shih found a kindred spirit in Prof Phang. They both believed that NUS students needed to be prepared for entrepreneurship, and Prof Phang had the entrepreneurial chops for the job. His founding of SEMICAPS, to conduct semiconductor failure analysis based on his research, made an impression on Prof Shih, and together they reached the same conclusion: Entrepreneurship cannot be taught in the classroom. It is a contact sport that must be learnt where the action takes place. This meant the students needed to intern with tech start-ups where the exposure would, hopefully, influence them to start new businesses.

There was another crucial factor: Stanford University and the University of California, Berkeley, both on the west coast of the US, had tech start-up hotspot Silicon Valley right in their midst as their reference while MIT, on the East Coast, had Route 128 to turn to. Singapore had none, which meant that students had to travel overseas to learn entrepreneurship, notably to the US and Europe where the phenomenon was prevalent.

NOC was what they would call their big hairy audacious goal or, in short, BHAG.

Achieving it, however, was an uphill task. The path was dotted with doubters and fence-sitters in NUS as well as outside, among government officials.

❝ They found it difficult to understand NOC and our aspirations even though we spelt out our vision," Prof Shih recalled. "It was not an easy sell for me. I could not point to an example of an enterprise anywhere that's like the NOC. ❞ [14]

To appreciate some of the challenges, one has to comprehend the NUS academic and social cultures in the early 2000s. In both areas, they were worlds apart from Silicon Valley, which drew throngs of self-confident entrepreneurs brimming with big ideas and capital. Coupled with its culture of exploration and experimentation, and the ability to face and accept failure, Silicon Valley became the crucible of such innovative companies as Google and Apple.

But the brief flashes of doubts in Singapore did not deter Prof Shih and Prof Phang. Instead, they viewed the challenges as opportunities for positive change.

Getting the buy-in from the NUS faculties, the NUS Board of Trustees and the Ministry of Education were critical because, among other things, the students needed approval from their respective faculty to participate in the new internship programme. The Ministry also wanted an assurance that NOC would not require additional funding from the government.

As stewards of NUS resources, the Trustees were naturally wary about spending money on a programme that did not have quantifiable outcomes in the foreseeable future, like the number of new start-ups that could be expected.

The two professors countered that that number would be meaningless. Global trends have shown that 90 per cent of start-ups failed. A start-up could close shop as easily as it opened. But the entrepreneurial skills learnt would not be lost, as they could be applied in all manner of businesses.

In any case, Prof Shih believed so strongly in the programme that he allocated about S$10 million, around one per cent of NUS' operating budget, to get NUS Enterprise[15] and NOC off the ground.

Another major challenge was student support. Among undergraduates, Prof Shih knew that the common ambition was to get a good degree and join the civil service or work in a multinational corporation. NOC, though, wanted risk-takers: students who aimed to do something different and out of their comfort zone. It was also necessary to separate them from those who merely wanted to have a fun time overseas.

Prof Jacob Phang (first from right) talking to NOC students.

No less worrisome was the fact that time away would delay the students' graduation. Besides, entrepreneurship was not a discipline like engineering and law. How would modules in entrepreneurship count towards their degree? This thorny issue of academic credits was tough to resolve, as the NUS Deans were largely opposed to accepting the courses the students would take at overseas universities as academic credits that counted towards their graduation.

They believed that entrepreneurship courses were either not an academic discipline or had no relevance for their students, and so had no place in their departments' curriculum. To overcome the roadblock, Prof Shih asked Associate Professor Wong Poh Kam, who was teaching at NUS Business School, to create the curriculum for an entrepreneurship minor programme. It would incorporate academic credits for both internship learning and entrepreneurship courses the NOC students would take.

NUS Business School, however, did not agree to accredit the new programme. This prompted Prof Shih to create a new teaching unit called the NUS Entrepreneurship Centre (NEC), with Prof Wong as the founding director. It was through this Centre that NOC students were

Professor Wong Poh Kam was the academic advisor for the NOC programme, and who helped NOC students to earn academic credits for their internship work.

Prof Teo Chee Leong (NOC Director 2002–2017) was well-known for his pre-departure pep talks to NOC students to prepare them for their NOC experience and as ambassadors for NUS.

able to receive academic credits for their internship learning and the entrepreneurship courses they took at overseas partner universities. Prof Wong played a central role in developing the entrepreneurship curriculum with the partner universities, as well as mentoring NOC entrepreneurs.[16]

After about 18 months, the basic outline of the NOC began to take shape.

To advance it, Prof Phang assembled the Entrepreneurship Task Force,[17] comprising himself, Adjunct Professor Dr Casey Chan,[18] Director, Industry and Technology Relations, Associate Professor Teo Chee Leong from the Faculty of Engineering, and Prof Wong to flesh out the details of the implementation. Additionally, a Working Committee was formed to provide strategic directions. The members came from the School of Computing, Faculty of Medicine, Faculty of Engineering, Faculty of Science and School of Business.

Running the NOC programme was an exhilarating experience for Prof Teo.

Prof Shih credited Prof Phang for leading a stellar team to roll out NOC.

> ❝ He was a hugely motivational and positive person. He communicated his passion and positive attitude in everything he did to his team. Everyone knew the larger purpose and the goals. NOC had never been done before anywhere else and everyone knew we had to find a way forward. It was like flying a plane and repairing it in flight. The runway was bumpy, there was turbulence in the air and headwind. The plane took off and kept flying — there was no turning back. Jacob was an able pilot. ❞

All the time, Prof Shih never took his eyes off the bigger picture: NUS' vital role in promoting entrepreneurship.

In his message in the NUS 2002 Annual Report, he wrote: "In an increasingly borderless world, knowledge is not pursued in isolation. Rather, it is advanced by a global community of scholars, researchers, and knowledge professionals, working together in social, professional and organisational networks. Indeed, creating, disseminating, and applying knowledge have become a global enterprise.

❝ In this global enterprise, the research university can play a critical role as catalyst for innovation and wealth creation. This is evident in the successful co-evolution of science and technology hubs alongside strong research universities in many parts of the world, including Silicon Valley and Route 128. They have leveraged on the natural synergies between education, research and entrepreneurship. ❞ [19]

To that end, Prof Shih set up NUS Enterprise to promote entrepreneurial activities and initiatives, and endeavour to instill an entrepreneurial culture at all levels of the NUS community. NOC was to be a key initiative under NUS Enterprise. Prof Phang was the founding Chief Executive Officer and NOC was officially formed with Prof Teo as the Founding Director.

By the end of 2001, the Entrepreneurship Task Force had agreed on the general framework. NOC's key features included:

- A 12-month overseas internship in tech hotspots. Prof Phang was insistent on the duration, saying that it was necessary to give the students time to settle in, learn and do something useful. The longer duration was a revolutionary idea at the time, but in hindsight, as much as any other reasons, it was instrumental in the success of NOC, said Prof Teo. Employers of interns liked the year-long internship because it enabled the students to work on major projects.

- Small, newly established start-ups were preferred as employers of NOC interns. They would give the students access to and learn directly from the founder-entrepreneurs on why they pursued a certain business strategy and did the things they did. The hope was for the interns to soak up the enthusiasm and spirit of these founders of tech start-ups and learn the importance of persistence and resilience. Also, the other employees might not be able to give a complete picture of decision-making in their firms.

- Interns were to be paid at least US$700 a month so that they would get meaningful jobs, ranging from doing market research and drawing up marketing plans to coding, customer support and pitching to investors. Also, what they produced would be implemented.

- During the internship, the students would take modules related to entrepreneurship at partner universities and earn academic credits for graduation from NUS.

The next task was to convince the faculties and schools to allow their students to go on the programme. They were very resistant to their students being away for a year and doing entrepreneurship courses they perceived as irrelevant to their major areas of studies. Prof Phang and Prof Teo made the rounds to convince them otherwise. On his part, Prof Shih would, whenever he joined the lengthy meetings, urge the Deans and academic staff to think of the upside of NOC. These included the students' exposure to another culture, experience of working in a start-up and taking classes with students from various parts of the world. **"Such an experience is invaluable and potentially transformative. Let's work to open new opportunities, new possibilities for our students,"** he would tell them.

Insider Help

Stanford University was the first partner university NOC negotiated with. While its top management supported the collaboration, the teaching staff were uncertain of the capabilities of NUS students. Enrolment was also full, and they did not want to teach additional students.

NUS, meanwhile, had found an ally in Professor Tom Kosnik, who taught at the Stanford Center for Professional Development and was a consulting professor at the Stanford Technology Ventures Program. Prof Wong had met him while on a sabbatical at Stanford in 2000, and Prof Kosnik subsequently became the important "insider" who aided NUS to get NOC going.

He helped the task force members navigate Stanford's management hierarchy and introduced them to various department heads who could influence the negotiation. He also included NUS students in the entrepreneurship class he was teaching. In addition, he drew up the first budget for the potential partnership. It would cost NUS about US$1.94 million from 2001 to 2004, an amount that could partly come out of the five-year grant of US$5 million[20] the National Science and Technology Board (NSTB)[21] gave NUS from the national R&D Fund. The rest could be taken from NUS' central budget.[22]

Prof Kosnik was strongly motivated by his belief that the collaboration would be a win-win for both. NUS was aspiring to be a world-class entrepreneurial university to aid Singapore's ambition to be the technopreneurial hub in Asia-Pacific. Stanford, on the other hand, was keen to learn how the NUS experience could be adapted and taught to other regions in the world. Both universities also wanted to globalise their students' educational experience through first-hand exposure to other countries' technopreneurial environments and interaction with students from other campuses.

In the winter of 2000, Professors Phang, Prof Wong and Prof Kosnik met at Stanford's Terman Building — named after Silicon Valley founder Frederick Terman — to discuss the final pieces of the tie-up. To earn the trust of Stanford's faculty, NUS students were required to take two to three modules on new venture creation, entrepreneurial marketing or technopreneurship. They had to maintain a B or B+ grade in their first module to continue taking classes at Stanford.

Finally, the BHAG envisioned by Prof Shih was within grasp. A Memorandum of Understanding was signed between NUS and Stanford in July 2001, with Prof Phang doing it in Singapore and two Stanford academics — Prof Elisabeth Paté-Cornell of the School of Engineering and Andy DiPaolo, the Executive Director of Stanford Center of Professional Development — in San Francisco.

CHAPTER 2

TURBULENT
Beginnings

Prof Shih looking resolutely ahead, steering NUS towards becoming a Global Knowledge Enterprise. He set up NUS Enterprise with NOC as a key initiative to instill a spirit of enterprise across the NUS community.

Lady Luck did not smile on the programme in the beginning. Before the NUS students could pack their bags and head for Silicon Valley in 2001, Al-Qaeda terrorists attacked the United States (US) on 11 September. Two passenger jets flew into the twin buildings of the World Trade Center which collapsed, killing thousands of people.

It was an earth-shaking start for the NOC.

Overnight, the US Embassy stopped issuing visas, said Prof Teo, who was the NOC Director at that time.

❝ We had to call the Head of the Consular Section of the US Embassy to convince her that NOC was a legitimate internship programme, that our students weren't going there to find work but to intern and study, and then return to Singapore to finish their final courses for a degree. ❞

The NOC team also had to contend with the dotcom bust of 2001, when over-speculation in internet stocks destroyed many start-ups.

Prof Teo and Mrs Tok Yu Ling, an NUS staffer, headed to Silicon Valley to find out if NOC was still feasible. **"The sense of doom and gloom was palpable,"** said Prof Teo. "Offices and buildings were empty. Businesses were down in the dumps. Start-ups did not believe that NOC would work as they were struggling and would have no time to mentor interns and no money to pay the students. One company founder told the duo: 'You want us to train your students and pay them as well? You must be kidding. We have the pick of the students from Berkeley and Stanford.'"

However, there was a silver lining. NOC's 12-month internship became a competitive advantage over the typical three- to four-month stints of American undergraduates. They could do much more for their employers.

As optimism returned, flyers and notices soliciting applications greeted students almost everywhere on the NUS campus. Slightly more than 50 students[23] applied for the inaugural batch to the Silicon Valley and 14 were successful. About 80 per cent of the applicants were from technical disciplines, such as computer science and computer engineering.

As entrepreneurship was difficult to assess, NOC struggled to produce the qualifying criteria. Eventually, the hierarchy was settled. Topping it was the students' competence in their field of study and their appetite for risks. Next came their activities outside academic classes. Were they volunteers? Had they set up their own mini business or taken part in business idea competitions? Ultimately, the selectors looked for that X factor: can the students think out of the box, and have the gumption to work in or launch a start-up, the desire to create something, and the abilities to do so?

Those picked had to attend a pre-departure session, during which Prof Teo would, among other things, stress the invaluable opportunity they were given, and to treasure, not trash, it. He likened it to the last comic strip of Calvin and Hobbes in which Calvin said to Hobbes, "Let's go exploring", after a snowstorm had blanketed the landscape and the world was all white, like a white blank page. Prof Teo urged them to fill the new page of their lives with meaningful entrepreneurial experiences.

He also reminded them that as representatives of NUS and Singapore, they should conduct themselves well. Last but not least, he told them that while they might not be the smartest in the host company, they could be, and should be, the most hardworking.

As these final touches were made, Mrs Tok[24], who had been appointed the programme's Silicon Valley Director, had arrived in San Francisco to set up NOC's office and gather the things the students would need to settle in quickly. The first group arrived in January 2002. It was perhaps inevitable that she became their "mummy" and agony aunt, handholding them through their stay, because for many, it was their first time in the US and living on their own for 12 months in a foreign country.

Sheltered Students and Salmon Fishing

Some lived such sheltered lives that they struggled to find their own accommodation and meals, and even to do their laundry. She helped many buy their first car and open bank accounts. **"I remember getting feedback that our students were napping after lunch. They ate a rice lunch which made them sleepy. My advice to them: eat a light lunch like a sandwich."**

Another facet of her job was to identify potential start-ups for future cohorts of interns. **"Initially, I went knocking on doors. It's like a sales job; knock on 100 doors and you get 10 replies, and we would be lucky if one took our students."** The fact that Singapore has a good reputation and there were government entities, like the Economic Development Board, operating there, helped. Some founders who took in students had dealings with Singapore and were familiar with NUS. Over time, as NOC's reputation grew, internships were easier to come by, she added. Some start-ups became "repeat customers" who would accept one to two interns yearly.

Among the first batch of NOC students was Shreyan Singh, who was studying computer science on a scholarship from PSA Corporation, Singapore's leading port business company.[25]

His internship at Buildfolio, an enterprise software company in California, was life-changing. In the first month, he was involved in software development and by the second month, he was meeting customers, a skill his computer science course would not have taught him. **"It wasn't the complexity of the work, but the ability to pull together multiple working parts to make something work."**

Currently a Managing Director of tech consultancy Accenture and looking after its Microsoft business activities, he said, "NOC changed my outlook on risk. I make very risky, weighted decisions about career, roles and organisations, and jobs. My bosses say I always seem to approach the job as if I were on my first day at work, with nothing to lose. They are surprised at this."

Over the years, NOC has grown from strength to strength. From almost 50 applications at the start, it now regularly attracts hundreds annually. Even during the Covid-stricken period of 2020, 636 applications were received.

Prof Phang, who, like a doting father, had watched NOC blossom, stepped down in 2006 from NUS Enterprise to focus on his academic work and SEMICAPS. Tragically, the entrepreneurial academician died from cancer in 2013 at age 60.

Tay Kae Fong, an NOC alumni who founded branding and design firm Binomial, echoed the sentiments of many NOC alumni when he said, in a tribute he wrote in the 9 January 2013 edition of start-up blog e27[26]: **"Prof Phang showed us by example what it meant to not accept roadblocks and to think beyond. He never took status quo as satisfactory and constantly challenged it to see how it can be better. Maybe, it's something everyone is used to now, but back in 2002, when the entrepreneurial mindset was new, it was liberating to know we could change anything we didn't like."**

The late Prof Jacob Phang, who had an illustrious career as a lecturer and scientist, rallied the NUS faculty and students to accept the overseas internship programme.

Wild salmon caught in the Pacific Ocean off Northern California on a fishing trip with NOC Silicon Valley interns in June 2002. Prof Shih (third from right) is with the fishing crew.

Prof Shih, similarly, rarely took his eyes off his "baby". In 2002, on a visit to San Francisco, he invited the interns on a salmon fishing trip in the Pacific Ocean. Ten turned up at 6am and they set off. This was their first time deep sea fishing. The seas were rough and soon, the students became seasick. They asked to return to shore but Prof Shih pushed on.

The trip finally turned into a roaring success as they caught about 40 large salmon, each weighing 15kg to 20kg.

Tay recounted:

" We smelt like fish, we were soaked although we wore waterproof jackets, but we had great salmon sashimi when we landed on Angel Island off San Francisco for lunch. "

Prof Shih Choon Fong took some of the first batch of NOC students in Silicon Valley on a salmon fishing trip in June 2002. The waters were choppy and several were sea sick, but they caught 40 salmon.

The lesson Prof Shih said he wanted to impress on them was that entrepreneurs face many challenges. But they must be resilient and persistent, and not give up the minute they face their first obstacle.

> ❝ I also wanted them to learn first-hand about the difference between pond and ocean fishing. When they graduate, I want them to fish in the rich ocean waters. They must know ocean fishing can be rough, but they can survive and thrive if they are determined. ❞

NOC Lifting Singapore Into Top 20 Start-Up Cities

Prof Phang was succeeded by Dr Lily Chan in February 2006. She had spent eight years in the venture capital industry as Managing Director of Investment at Bio*One Capital.[27]

With a sense of urgency, Dr Chan put her plans to work. One was to expand NOC's network of overseas locations to further foster entrepreneurship education. The other was to take the ongoing experiment to the next level by nurturing entrepreneurship development.

Dr Lily Chan expanded the NOC programme to more locations worldwide and extended the BLOCK71 entrepreneurial ecosystem initiative to Indonesia.

A crucial stimulus for building the community was networking sessions, which NUS Enterprise introduced and held initially at its office in the Kent Ridge Campus. These sessions, at which the NOC alumni mingled with investors, entrepreneurs and corporate executives, were expanded in 2011 to BLOCK71, Singapore's first building established specifically for the country's tech start-up community.

The get-togethers became a regular and popular event. The informal setting was conducive for sharing knowledge, building contacts and finding co-founders and business partners for their projects. But the major crowd-puller was the talks given by well-known investors and start-up stars like Airbnb co-founder Brian Chesky and Kickstarter co-founder Charles Adler.

BLOCK71 was central to the success of the mission. It became the embodiment of the traditional office water cooler where the tenants, comprising entrepreneurs, investors, start-up accelerators and new tech companies, could get acquainted or meet informally over a cuppa to share information.

Dr Chan, referencing a physics concept, said that the place brought to mind the Brownian motion, which states that particles suspended in a liquid or gas move in a random fashion. **"If we didn't aggregate this community, they will be all over the place and never get a chance to meet, to get to know each other, and there will be less synergy."**

She went on to offer:

❝ Entrepreneurship is a lonely profession. It is good for them to know there is support from the community, and fellow sufferers give them hope, too. ❞

The mission to add new NOC locations was, however, a less smooth journey.

Dr Chan had eyed the possibility of adding London to the initial list that comprised Silicon Valley and Philadelphia in the US, and the German city of Munich. But after discussions with Prof Teo and Prof Wong, she dropped the idea. There were too many distractions in London, she said.

❝ The students know too much about the country and the city, and they will be running all over the place enjoying themselves instead of focusing on NOC. ❞

Also, London was unlike Silicon Valley, **"where in any Starbucks outlet you would find start-up founders sitting and doing work,"** she added.

Another tough destination was Israel. The start-up founders she spoke to wanted to be paid to teach the NUS students entrepreneurship. But under the NOC programme, only the universities would be paid for courses taken by the NUS students. Her argument: When start-ups take **"our interns, they are going to provide them with work, they become part of the team, and so they should be paid."** After an extensive search, a few were found among the thousands in the country, and in 2011, NOC was launched in Israel.

One location that proved particularly difficult was Bangalore, the tech hub of India. The "hardship" stemmed from the difficulty in getting around, finding comfortable lodgings and being paid acceptable wages.

As a result, the stint was reduced from 12 to three months, although some students extended it to six months. The issue of safety for the women interns finally led Dr Chan to abandon Bangalore.

Crucial to the success of the locations was money. She turned to public sector agencies like SPRING Singapore,[28] and their contributions[29] helped NUS Enterprise maintain a budget that remained more or less the same during her 13-year term.

The agencies, however, leaned towards deep tech start-ups, which focus on such technologies as artificial intelligence, blockchain, advanced material science and quantum computing. The NOC students, on the other hand, tended to launch consumer tech companies. **"I knew that if I had just relied on deep tech alone, we would not have seen the start-up growth that actually happened."**

She said:

> 66 Gone are the days when you can make one striking invention and stay successful for decades — like the 3M sticky pads. It's just one technology. Today's deep tech companies require an amalgamation and aggregation of technologies to become successful. 99

Dr Chan was spurred to pursue two routes of potential success. One was to license the intellectual property of NUS researchers to deep tech companies. The other was to give the NOC students room to explore.

> 66 Let them make something of the Brownian motion, let as many of them create start-ups as possible. Surely, one would work. And we were right. There was tenCube, Zopim and others, and they were acquired, showing the NOC alumni had built good businesses. 99

Deep tech start-ups, incidentally, also required greater funding in the order of millions of dollars, she noted. **"Investors during my early years at NUS Enterprise were reluctant to part with S$1 million or S$2 million because they had not seen anything successful emerging from the Singapore start-up ecosystem."**

Today, they are more willing. Tens of millions, if not hundreds of millions, of dollars have flowed into several NOC and other Singapore start-ups, including PatSnap, founded by NOC alumni to provide intellectual property and R&D intelligence; and Grab, Southeast Asia's leading superapp that provides everyday services such as deliveries, mobility and financial services. Listed on the New York Stock Exchange in 2021, Grab led a consortium that was among the winners of Malaysia's digital banking licenses in April 2022.

Dr Chan left NUS Enterprise in March 2019, by which time NOC had been lauded for contributing to Singapore becoming an important start-up node in the world. Singapore was ranked 14th globally in Startup Genome's 2019 annual start-up ecosystem report.[30] Only two other Asian cities are in the top 20: Beijing in the third spot and Shanghai in eighth.

After 20 years, about 3,600 NUS students have imbibed the entrepreneurial lessons. The NOC network has more than 15 overseas locations, spread out in the US, Canada, Europe and Asia, including Southeast Asia. Also, many of the interns have become successful entrepreneurs, with some working in the start-up ecosystem as investors and mentors, and others in the innovation ecosystem.

The BHAG envisioned by Prof Shih had been achieved.

CHAPTER 3

BUILDING A
Start-up
Ecosystem

A bird's eye view of Blk71.

It was almost a daily ritual for Michael Yap.

Before starting work, the Deputy Chief Executive Officer (CEO) of the Media Development Authority (MDA)[31] would stand at the floor-to-ceiling windows of his office on the 16th floor of Symbiosis, Fusionopolis, to gaze at the panoramic view of Ayer Rajah and beyond. The view helped to clear his thoughts.

But on a particular morning in 2010, a cluster of dilapidated buildings in the distance captured his attention and set him thinking.

He had been wrestling for weeks with the problem of how to help fledgling tech start-ups — especially those that received grants from a government micro-financing scheme — to overcome a particularly searing challenge: Soaring office rents.

"It gave me sleepless nights." One possibility he envisioned was for the MDA to lease a building, retrofit it with offices and rent them to the start-ups at budget-friendly prices. **"I just needed to find the right building."**

That building, it dawned on him on that sunny April morning, could be tucked in the rundown cluster he had spotted in Ayer Rajah Industrial Estate.

Built in the early 1970s for manufacturers to test, assemble and package products, the buildings had fallen into disuse and disrepair.

Though due for demolition by 2020, the cluster was not without historical significance. There, at a building called Blk67, was where Creative Technology, one of Singapore's early tech superstars, spent part of its fledgling years in the 1990s.

Almost 30 years later another among them would be picked to play a history-making role. It was Blk71.

The seven-storey building was vacant and was slated for demolition in 2010. The paint was peeling, almost every hinge joint and window grille were coated with rust and creepy-crawlies had turned the empty premises into their playground and home.

Michael Yap, deputy CEO of MDA, saw in the unused flatted factory building called Blk71 an opportunity to create a focal point for the start-up ecosystem to meet and network.

When NOC offered its proposed plan, Jurong Town Corporation (JTC), the Government's developer of industrial infrastructure, agreed to delay the demolition. Instead it retrofitted the building, reinventing it into one of the world's densest start-up ecosystems and the beacon of Singapore's digital ambitions.

But the transformative journey was not led by Yap alone. He had joined forces with two others: Dr Lily Chan, chief executive of NUS Enterprise, and Yvonne Kwek, chief executive of Singtel's new venture arm, Innov8.

The tireless trio had a common vision: to gather people, ideas and funds at a focal point where the interactions and encounters among the prospective inventors could create synergy that results in new ventures and innovations.

Their teaming up was in itself fortuitous. Each had separately grappled with similar problems.

Yap's major task was to find physical space for digital media start-ups that had received grants of up to S$50,000 from a national micro-financing scheme to prove their ideas were doable. This i.JAM Fund, managed by the inter-agency Interactive Digital Media Programme Office, is aimed at encouraging innovation and entrepreneurship.

Dr Chan, meanwhile, was fretting over the lack of space the NUS Enterprise Incubator provides for incubator companies at various on-campus locations such as the Prince George's Park bungalows and the School of Computing. The squeeze threatened to retard the successful NOC programme's bid to demonstrate that entrepreneurship can be nurtured. She had scouted various locations to replace Prince George's Park, including abandoned schools and an old factory in the Commonwealth area, buildings in Singapore Science Park and even a factory block in Ayer Rajah Industrial Estate.

As CEO NUS Enterprise, Dr Lily Chan played a key role in developing the BLOCK71 entrepreneurial initiative. Together with Michael Yap, deputy CEO of MDA, and Yvonne Quek, CEO of Singtel Innov8, they turned the industrial building into a start-up hub.

> **❝ I had several meetings with Yap about the factory block in Ayer Rajah Industrial Estate. We'd also discussed inviting a venture fund as a collaborator to develop BLOCK71 into the start-up focal point for Singapore. ❞**

At Innov8, Kwek was intent on finding an office space away from Singtel's corporate offices. Innov8 was formed in 2010 to focus on disruptive new technologies and she believed that it was best to adopt a structure dissimilar to that of Singtel. An office away from Singtel would reinforce that.

Amid her search, she was contacted by Dr Chan in 2010 about collaborating on BLOCK71. The duo hit it off instantly, drawn by their shared goal to build a start-up ecosystem.

Yap, meanwhile, had identified two blocks in Ayer Rajah Industrial Estate. **"They had character because they were used for economic purposes; previously, it was manufacturing, now it's tech disruption."**

His plan was to lease at least one block and rent the office space to digital media start-ups. To jumpstart it, he turned to Dr Chan as a tie-up with NUS Enterprise would promise a pipeline of start-ups from among the alumni of NOC as well as NUS.

> **❝ They were crucial because we needed a group of folks who would undertake activities to nurture and promote start-ups without being over-constrained by profit considerations. Also, such a critical mass was key to creating synergy and securing financial feasibility. ❞**

Over time, these moves proved to be vital. For years, the government had supported digital innovations. But Singapore had never taken the step to develop a start-up ecosystem prior to 2000, a place where believers can congregate and live their dream to innovate.

Together, the trio was to pioneer the framework for the ecosystem. Yap became the landlord, leasing five floors out of the seven in the building for three years; Dr Chan would develop events for the tech community besides providing the pipeline of start-ups; and Kwek, the provider of funds, would financially support eligible companies.

The journey, however, was anything but smooth. Getting JTC Corp to lease space was an uphill task, Yap recalled. The flatted factories in the Ayer Rajah Estate were part of the 200 hectare One North Masterplan. They were about 40 years old in 2010 and the plan was to tear them down by 2020 and redevelop the area into an innovation and technopreneurship hub comprising business parks, laboratories and commercial office space.

Measures were already underway. A nearby building called Blk73 had been demolished and tenants' leases were being renewed on a three-year basis in view of the 2020 deadline. The only available building was Blk71 but retrofitting and leasing it for just 10 years would not be economically viable, JTC insisted.

After lengthy discussions over several months, Yap convinced JTC that a basic retrofit was good enough for an experiment on providing affordable office space to budding start-ups.

A three-year lease of five floors was inked in 2011, with JTC managing the remaining two floors. MDA subsidised the rents, making them cheaper than the surrounding office spaces. The rents were about S$2 per sq. ft, which was about half the commercial rates in the area. Offices with air-conditioning were available at $2.50 per sq. ft.

The next big hurdle was the operational details.

Dr Chan and Kwek had two demands: sitting toilets and lights. They had stepped out into the dark night after long meetings and were concerned about safety for the tenants.

Lights were introduced along the pathways to Fusionopolis, across the road from BLOCK71, and the main roads of Ayer Rajah Crescent and Ayer Rajah Avenue. Squat toilets were replaced, every wall and ceiling refreshed with a coat of white paint, lifts upgraded and general repairs carried out. Kwek coaxed Singtel to give the building free wireless connection. The minimal retrofitting was completed in a few months.

Other requests, however, took years. For instance, hot water showers in the toilets for entrepreneurs, developers and engineers who work late were not met for several years.

The final detail was the building's name, which can become a rallying point for the start-up community. Everyone agreed that it must call to mind tech start-ups in Singapore and their suggestions included One North Valley and Silicon Loop. But Dr Chan objected, noting there was no valley or silicon in Singapore.

While brainstorming, an Innov8 executive called Aaron Tan proposed a name that was right under their noses. He recounted that daily, he would instruct the cabby driving him to work to take him to BLOCK71 Ayer Rajah. Both Dr Chan and Kwek loved the moniker, noting it was very Singaporean as few countries referred to their buildings as blocks. Also, it brings to mind geeky techies.

With that settled, the building opened its doors in March 2011. Innov8 and NUS Enterprise moved in in September that year, sharing an open office space on the second floor. NUS Enterprise ran another co-working space next to this office, called Plug-In@Blk71.

The decor was starkly industrial, with each floor uniformly lit by white fluorescent lights and rooms with rows of new desks and chairs pushed against the walls like in a classroom.

Still, it represented a pioneering effort as small start-ups could rent space by the number of desks rather than by area. They shared facilities such as the pantry, meeting rooms and a sitting area.

In no time, BLOCK71, as it is spelt, became a distinctive name and today it is known globally, with *The Economist* weekly magazine referring to it as the world's most tightly packed entrepreneurial ecosystem.

But the endeavour was not without growing pains. From the start, it was put through a real life proof of concept (POC) and proof of value (POV) exercise.

In the first six months, the NUS Enterprise team, with landlord MDA, used subsidised rental and furnishing grants to lure potential tenants. Still, start-ups did not bite.

Is location the problem, wondered Gang Chern Sun, who is currently senior associate director, BLOCK71 Singapore. A flatted factory in an industrial estate with the lingering smell of oil and grime symbolises a fading era, in sharp contrast to the chic colours and sleek interiors of the offices of tech giants such as Facebook and Google. Never mind that these behemoths started in university dormitories or home bedrooms and moved to garages; posh surroundings seemed like a basic requirement for attracting start-ups.

A little voice in Gang, however, told him to heed his own start-up experience, which informed him that entrepreneurs yearned to be around like-minded individuals with whom they could share ideas, ask questions and network.

Therein lies the rub: no such community existed in Singapore in 2011 as start-ups and investment companies were dispersed across Singapore. So he set about building one at BLOCK71. Working together with Dr Chan, he boosted the calendar of events, with talks by successful entrepreneurs and technologists, networking sessions with investors and corporate executives, hackathons and various tech activities.

Topping his list of guest speakers were the likes of Brian Chesky, co-founder, Airbnb; Charles Adler, co-founder, Kickstarter; Scott Guthrie, Executive Vice President, Microsoft; Mark Chang, founder, JobStreet and many others. Their knowledge was invaluable for start-ups building mobile solutions.

Soon, word spread that BLOCK71 was where a start-up could meet coders, engineers and fellow entrepreneurs. Start-ups and venture capital firms were captivated and in just over a year, the building was almost full.

Its early tenants included well-known NOC start-ups such as Carousell, food discovery site Burpple and 99.co, as well as other companies like educational technology start-up KooBits founded by an NUS alumni and venture capital firm Stream Global. Carousell began by renting desks at NUS Enterprise's co-working space. Its co-founder Quek Siu Rui, an NOC alumni, found it beneficial to sit next to other entrepreneurs because it allowed them to discuss and share information.

One day in 2013, he unexpectedly found himself sitting next to NOC serial entrepreneur Darius Cheung, co-founder of property portal 99.co and whose earlier company tenCube had been acquired by American antivirus software pioneer McAfee of the United States (US) for an undisclosed eight-figure sum.

Quek, who was then aged 26 while Darius was 32, recalled being overwhelmed. **"He's my hero. My co-founders and I were then so young; we did not know anything. We would ask him for help, for even simple things like what an employee contract form should look like. The next minute, it's in our email."**

Stream Global's managing partner Chak Kong Soon, who was enticed by the ecosystem, noted that every 10 steps would lead entrepreneurs to the door of a venture capital firm. **"The vibrancy was palpable,"** he said.

Outside, the car park that had been empty in 2011 soon had drivers waiting 15 minutes or longer for a parking space, and before long, it was dotted with shiny new luxury cars and SUVs.

The dramatic turnaround can be credited to the buzz created by news of tech buyouts and newly-minted young millionaires as well as the presence of well-heeled investors and venture capitalists.

When McAfee bought tenCube in August 2010, it made four struggling NOC alumni in their 20s instant multimillionaires. A month later, another Singapore-based start-up, Viki, an online entertainment service, was acquired by Japanese e-commerce giant Rakuten for US$200 million.

Singapore venture fund, Neoteny Labs, provided seed funding to Viki which was founded in 2007 by American Razmig Hovaghimian and Korean husband and wife team, Changseong Ho and Jiwon Moon. The buyouts gave a tremendous boost to Singapore's fledgling start-up ecosystem.

To ride the wave of interest, Singapore's first accelerator programme was launched in 2011 at BLOCK71. The first programme was sponsored by Innov8 and included participation by Singtel's regional associates in Indonesia, the Philippines, Thailand and India. Typically, an accelerator programme is about six months long and it supports early-stage start-ups through education, mentorship and financing.

Wong Meng Weng, co-founder of JFDI, decorated Plug-in@Blk71 with plants, improving the work environment.

Wong Meng Weng, co-founder of JFDI, had built and sold start-ups.

The programme was organised by Joyful Frog Digital Innovation (JFDI), a private-sector start-up accelerator that played an instrumental role in fostering activities at BLOCK71 and contributed to the growth of Singapore's start-up ecosystem.

It was set up in Singapore in 2010 by two techies: Briton Hugh Mason and Singaporean Wong Meng Weng. Mason was a science TV producer and entrepreneur in England as well as an MDA media consultant who would regularly visit Singapore in the 2000s, while technologist and inventor Wong was an entrepreneur who sold his successful start-ups in the US in the 2000s and returned home in 2009 after about 12 years in the US.

Following a rigorous selection process, eight start-ups were selected for the three-month programme, during which JFDI invited corporate executives to mentor entrepreneurs, venture capitalists to give talks and technologists to share their expertise. **"We wanted to build a community that is a safe space and allows lateral thinking and out of the box approaches,"** said Mason.

It culminated in a graduation ceremony called Demo Day, when the participants would demonstrate their products and pitch their ideas to investors for funds to build their business.

But before setting up JFDI at BLOCK71, the two men had been involved in developing a makerspace for engineers, technologists and hobbyists to tinker in a shophouse in Bussorah Street since 2009. The not-for-profit HackerspaceSG became a magnet for aficionados of computers, technology and science, as well as digital and electronic art to meet, socialise and collaborate. Built by geeks for geeks to tinker, it had facilities such as a 3D printer, a probe that measured Internet connectivity in real time and different types of microprocessor development boards.

Their vision was to resonate with a practice familiar in Singapore like eating frog porridge, a relatively common dish in Chinese cuisine. Hence, the frog became their symbol.

Hugh Mason, co-founder of JFDI, is a serial entrepreneur and start-up mentor.

The activities of HackerspaceSG reached the ears of Yap, who visited the duo, liked what they were doing and wanted JFDI to do the same at BLOCK71. JFDI moved into a small space in BLOCK71, squeezed between NUS Enterprise and Innov8. Its first accelerator programme started on the fourth day of Chinese New Year 2012.

From the start, the duo brought an air of *joie de vivre* to BLOCK71. First to go was the harsh clinical appearance, as two trucks arrived with 40 plants, each as tall as an average Singaporean adult. The desks and chairs were rearranged for the plants to be tucked between them, creating a "jungle-like" look. The fluorescent lights were replaced by IKEA table lamps.[32] Instantly, the office appeared happier and warmer.

Within months, the space became cramped. JFDI was pushed to move up to a 2,000 sq. ft space on an upper floor for its growing list of activities. They also introduced a cafe at the office entrance where a barista offered a choice of latte, capuccino or tea. It was also to accommodate the many coffee drinkers from the various offices who would throng its cafe for their morning shot and tea break. Like the water cooler in the past that boosted productivity, its cafe promotes cohesion and collaboration, even among seeming rivals.

Looking back at the swift success, Gang said that the BLOCK71 experiment played a crucial role in catalysing the country's tech start-up industry, which, in turn, helped bolster Singapore's development as a knowledge economy.

It also crystallised NUS' role in promoting entrepreneurship, **"showing that as a university, we had the risk appetite to take on such an experiment"**.

He, however, was quick to add that he and his team were principally guided by the belief that it was easier to fail quickly, that is, to introduce new ways of doing things and change quickly if they do not work out.

"We operated like a start-up. We were given a blank canvas. All three stakeholders — Michael, Lily and Yvonne — gave us maximum autonomy. As our parents, they supported us with resources."

Wong Meng Weng (left) and Hugh Mason of Joyful Frog Digital Innovation held network gatherings, meet-ups and pitching sessions, vastly aiding the start-up development in Singapore. The frog is JFDI's mascot.

Like a proud, achieving child, he added:

❝ We'd turned BLOCK71 into a one-stop start-up hub. Every day, an event or two is being held. In the past, founders, who wanted to do something related to start-ups, had to go to different places to look for talent, knowledge and community. Now, everything is consolidated at BLOCK71. ❞

BLOCK71 in Ayer Rajah Industrial Estate has been described by The Economist *in 2014 as the world's most tightly packed entrepreneurial ecosystem.*

By end-2012, media reports on a "thriving hub" for start-ups called BLOCK71 were making the headlines in Singapore's main newspaper, *The Straits Times*, and soon after it was featured in prestigious publications such as *The New York Times* daily newspaper and *The Economist* magazine.

By 2015, BLOCK71 boasted the largest cluster of start-ups in Singapore. Prof Tan Chorh Chuan, NUS President between 2008 and 2017, said that BLOCK71 led to a community that was self-supporting where entrepreneurs, investors and others in the start-up community helped each other. For NUS, it was about carrying out its aim of encouraging entrepreneurship.[33]

BLOCK71 was a way for NUS **"to convert the NOC one-year experience into a longer-term support system to aid those who wanted to pursue entrepreneurship"**.

Crisis at BLOCK71

But a threat soon emerged in 2013. MDA, as the master tenant, decided to pull the plug on the "i.JAM Fund" experiment, a microfunding scheme to support entrepreneurs to validate their start-up ideas. This meant that MDA was giving up the lease for the five floors and returning it to JTC. The start-ups on these five floors were left in the lurch.

For JTC, the departure of MDA left it at a crossroad. It either took over the management of the whole building and continued to develop it as a start-up space or reverted to the original plan and tore it down to build commercial buildings and business parks as part of the One North development plans.

While mulling over the options, JTC extended the tenants' lease by one year.

Its then CEO Png Cheong Boon was cognizant of the fact that dispersing the incubators and start-ups across Singapore would inhibit the movement's growth.

History has shown that start-ups need a focal point for believers to gather and nourish each other as they share their ideas, woes and wins. The rise of Silicon Valley and, closer to home, Bangalore in India, testify to that.

But as Png grappled with the issue, the contract of those with three-year leases required them to move out in the first quarter of 2015. It was a crisis for BLOCK71, marking a possible death knell for the experiment.

These soaring figures were not lost on Png, who moved swiftly to expand on the concept of BLOCK71 and meet the inevitable demand for more space. He resurrected Blk73, which had been torn down in 2010, as a three-storey building. Blk79 was added and together, the cluster of three formed a newly-created special zone for tech start-ups. It was named JTC LaunchPad @ one-north. A basketball and a futsal court were added to ensure that life for techies was not all work and no play.

"We wanted to do it quickly because start-ups can't wait a few years for new buildings. By then, they might have closed down. As they say, time, tide and technology wait for no man."

Coincidentally, JTC was also experimenting with new building construction methods that involve no piling but with structures stacked one on top of the other. As a result, a building could be completed in nine months. In the case of Blocks 73 and 75, JTC got them up and ready in a record eight months.

In addition, LaunchPad offered discounted rents, which were lower than those of nearby commercial offices, but the start-ups were required to be younger than three years. Eligible start-ups could renew their lease for another three years as well.

The policy ensured what the industry called churn, a continual turnover of tenants as new start-ups were able to get a space with relative ease and keep the ecosystem fresh.

In January 2015, Prime Minister Lee Hsien Loong opened LaunchPad and gave BLOCK71 a pat on the back. **"I'm very happy that BLOCK71 has been successful. There are now 1,200 people working in 260 start-ups and 25 incubators."**[34]

By end-2017, another three blocks were added. The concept, proven successful, has been replicated for other industries. In Jurong, an enclave called LaunchPad @ Jurong Innovation District was set up for cleantech, comprising advanced manufacturing, urban solutions and engineering start-ups.

BLOCK71 also spread its wings overseas, with an offshoot set up in San Francisco in 2015. The 5,000 sq. ft space was created to help Singaporean start-ups get a foothold in Silicon Valley.

Several overseas offers soon landed on the lap of Dr Chan. They were offers to franchise the concept of BLOCK71 in other countries. To her, BLOCK71 is not just a building for tech start-ups to rent. Its success is the combination of hardware, that is the building, and the NUS Enterprise "software" comprising the networking activities, the tenant mix and the giant water cooler culture that allowed people to mix, ideas to aggregate and new businesses to emerge.

The "software" could not be franchised. However, overseas expansion is beneficial for NOC/NUS and Singapore start-ups because it has a self-supporting system to promote entrepreneurship.

Dr Chan then decided that the expansion of BLOCK71 would be one of partnership. NUS Enterprise would link up with an overseas partner in a country, one with links to the tech start-up community. NUS Enterprise would bring its know-how of community engagement and development and entrepreneurship mentoring.

In this way, other BLOCK71s were soon set up in Yogyakarta and Bandung in Indonesia, Hanoi in Vietnam, Suzhou in China and Nagoya in Japan. These act as staging points for NOC as well as Singapore start-ups to expand into the region and opportunities to network with local entrepreneurs, investors and others in the start-up community.

On 21 August 2016, Prime Minister Lee, in his annual National Day Rally address, endorsed the success of BLOCK71,

In 2015, Prime Minister Lee Hsien Loong (third from left) opened LaunchPad @ one north which included BLOCK71. Attendees at the opening include Dr Lily Chan, then CEO of NUS Enterprise (left) and Prof Tan Eng Chye, (second from left), current President of NUS.

❝ It started with a small group of start-ups. It has been very successful. Now, it has expanded to Block 73 and Block 79. So now they have changed the name and they have called it JTC LaunchPad. We even have a BLOCK71 in San Francisco to help our start-ups tap the United States market and the Silicon Valley network. ❞

Then with a touch of caution, he added: **"It is still early days, but it looks promising. The start-ups are growing, and investors are paying attention... maybe the next Google, Facebook or Alibaba may come from Singapore."**

STAGE 2

THE
BENEFICIARIES

CHAPTER 4

THE UNICORNS: PATSNAP:
All about IP Intelligence

PatSnap is one of NOC's successes. It was founded by two NOC alumni, Jeffrey Tiong and Guan Dian.

In his oversized T-shirt and with hair down to his shoulders, Jeffrey Tiong was — by his own admission — "looking very unreliable" as he strode in his slippers into BLooiE's Roadhouse Bar & Grill on a cool evening in December 2009.

He was to meet a potential business partner to help him take his fledgling start-up PatSnap to the next level. The search engine-like portal, which taps on artificial intelligence and machine learning, provides data and analytics for innovators.

He met his friend who, as promised, had brought along Guan Dian to meet him at the Kent Ridge eatery. Like Tiong, Guan was an NOC alumni. They had never met but the solidarity from their common past sparked a comfortable familiarity that fuelled their conversation for the next three hours. By the end of the night, she was ready to join forces with him.

Did his scrappy appearance make her chary? She hardly remembers it, saying with a smile:

“ What I do remember of that meeting was heading home with a feeling of excitement that I'd be joining a start-up full of challenges.”

She was then 21 years old and Tiong, 26.

That meeting has turned out to be serendipitous, with PatSnap — short for Patents in a Snap — crowned a unicorn in 2021. It is the first National University of Singapore (NUS)-supported unicorn and joins an elite group of companies in the region that includes e-commerce platform Lazada and the decacorn, multiservice app Grab.

Founded in 2007, PatSnap, however, had minimal success in its first two years. Tiong had launched it right after graduating from the NUS Engineering Faculty and the following year, moved the business from Singapore to China. But it did not take off as expected.

Today, he believes that bringing Guan on board was the catalyst that propelled the business.

> 66 I was aware that I couldn't do everything myself. I needed a partner to build and take the venture to the next level. 99

Now based in Suzhou, China's second-largest industrial city, PatSnap is a far cry from the company he started with a S$55,000 grant from Singapore's Media Development Authority (MDA).[35] Guan was then a newly-minted NUS graduate in computing who had her sights set firmly on working in a start-up. Like Tiong, her NOC experience in the United States (US) had left an indelible mark. When she heard that he was keen on boosting his operations in China, she asked their mutual friend to set up the fateful meeting.

Both acknowledged that their shared link with NOC was a major factor that brought them together. They understood each other's motivations, were unafraid of failure and welcomed challenges as part and parcel of growing a start-up. As Guan declares proudly, those who have been through the vigorous process are in a "special club".

"It completely changes your mindset," explained the 36-year-old who lives in Shanghai and is PatSnap's Senior Vice President of Asia-Pacific and a key founding team member. **"You feel like you can accomplish anything, and everything can be a possibility if you ONLY dare to dream. Both of us may have been naive, but that entrepreneurial spirit helped us push through the hardships and focus on what we wanted to do with PatSnap."**

Once in a Lifetime Opportunity

The NOC programme has been a game changer for many of its participants, often upending their earlier career ambitions. Tiong, as a biomedical engineering student, had envisioned a career as an engineer working 9am to 5pm, while Guan's dream was to work in a bank. But following their stint in the US, both unhesitatingly changed course.

Tiong's spell, in 2005, was in Bio Valley, Philadelphia. He interned at a medical device company, BioConnect Systems, and studied part-time at the University of Pennsylvania's famed Wharton School. He stayed another six months as he felt the 12-month stint did not give him the degree of exposure he wanted. Born in Sabah, the naturalised Singaporean was 21 when he left for the US.

Guan, however, was born in the Chinese province of Sichuan and came to Singapore to study at age 17. In her first year at university, she joined the NUS Entrepreneurship Society (NES), which offers members opportunities to network and learn from people in the Singapore business community. Often, she would hear them talk admiringly of the NOC programme. In 2007, she successfully applied for it and at age 20, she was off to Silicon Valley. There, she interned as a coder for video tech company MooWee and did classes at Stanford University.

More than a decade has passed since their NOC days, but the duo still reminisce about the lessons learnt and the joy of starting a business to solve problems. As interns, they attended talks by big names in the start-up scene such as Scott McNealy, the co-founder of Sun Microsystems, and Amazon's Jeff Bezos.

The duo also went to events where they mingled with local investors and took part in competitions to pitch ideas to investors.

Tiong, who was selected for the NOC programme on his second try, said:

66 When we met founders of start-ups, there was no hierarchy. They willingly shared the successes and setbacks of their businesses. I had read, since young, so much about the US tech ecosystem and Silicon Valley, but you have to experience it for yourself to know how impactful it is. 99

Most NOC alumni agree that the programme is only as good as the effort put in by the participant, and that includes trying things outside their comfort zones.

Tiong took part in the prestigious Wharton Business Plan Competition, in which teams, with at least one undergraduate or graduate student from the University of Pennsylvania, pitch potential business ideas to judges from the business and venture capital community. Their proposals were scrutinised, analysed and taken apart as the investors looked for the next big thing to plough their money into.

He was the first NOC intern to take part in the competition and made it to the final list of eight teams that presented their ideas to a theatre filled with hundreds of people, including investors, faculty and students.

> **It was something extra that I wanted to do, on top of my classes and job. Though I didn't win, it was a great opportunity to compete with people with great ideas and to network.**

With his new-found confidence, he set up PatSnap. The idea originated from his NOC internship, during which he had to handle patents and intellectual property matters. He noticed the company's engineers and scientists were spending long hours sieving through legal data because there was no efficient system for patent analytics. The tedious search process was also expensive. To simplify it, he tinkered with producing an efficient patent search engine.

He began developing the concept while finishing his last semester at NUS and lost no time in making it a reality when he graduated.

> ❝ If it fails, it fails. It would be no big deal. NOC gave me that confidence and blissful ignorance to go for it. I thought start-up life was cool and it would be easy. ❞

Besides the S$55,000 from MDA, PatSnap also received incubation support from NUS Enterprise. Still, it was a struggle to get it off the ground. In the first six months, he would shower and sleep in his office at Prince George's Park on NUS campus and took home a monthly salary of no more than S$500. When he moved to Suzhou in 2008, he worked out of an apartment that he shared with his team of seven. In winter, they would turn off the heater to save money.

When Guan joined PatSnap, she moved in with them and they got by with just the bare essentials. The neighbourhood they lived in was dodgy but the rent was relatively low. She got around on a second-hand electric scooter and worked daily till the wee hours of the morning. But dealing with the tough living conditions was the easy part, she said.

> ❝ It was nothing compared to the mental stress of growing PatSnap. We had no money and had to build business connections from scratch. Often, while we were trying to come up with new product prototypes, we would set deadlines but at times, there would be nothing to show. Still, we went to potential clients and pitched, despite knowing it wasn't good. I felt frustrated like I had failed the customers' trust. ❞

She added with a laugh:

> **❝** Those were the hard parts — feeling mentally stressed rather than dealing with the physical discomforts. But entrepreneurs are optimistic people. If we knew how hard it would be, we wouldn't have started. **❞**

Pushing Past Setbacks

Like the successful American tech titans who shared their trials and tribulations in building their companies, the duo never lost heart. As Tiong describes PatSnap on his LinkedIn page, **"Similar to Q who provides all the high-tech gadgets to James Bond to fight the bad guys on the frontline, we hope to be the Q to innovators' James Bond!"**

Along the way, they received help. When PatSnap was branching out in China, the company was supported by the NUS Suzhou Research Institute and BLOCK71.

In 2010, with a few clients like Singapore's Agency for Science, Technology and Research (A*STAR), PatSnap had a breakthrough: when venture capital firm Accel-X and NUS Enterprise invested US$900,000 in it.[36] The move to China was starting to pay off. The following year, Guan brought in PatSnap's first Chinese clients.

Since then, it has become one of the fastest growing big data software-as-a-service (SaaS) companies, with offices in Singapore, the US, China and England. The company has about 800 employees across three continents and a 10,000-strong client list that includes notable organisations such as Tesla, Dyson, NASA and Xiaomi. It has also received the seal of approval from mega investors such as Japanese tech conglomerate SoftBank's Vision Fund 2 and Chinese powerhouse Tencent Investment.

The duo, meanwhile, have become the prized poster children for the start-up movement in Singapore, earning accolades and mentions as outstanding technopreneurs.

In 2017, Tiong won the NUS Outstanding Young Alumni Award for his achievements and outstanding contributions to his chosen field. The following year, he won the EY Entrepreneur Of The Year for Singapore.[37] Ernst & Young, a global leader in assurance, consulting as well as tax services in more than 50 countries, gives the award annually to entrepreneurs around the world for their achievements in demonstrating vision, leadership and success. In 2020, Tiong was named a Top 50 SaaS CEO by The Software Report, the established New York City-based market research firm that reports on market developments, corporate actions, investment activity and executive insights related to the software industry.[38]

Guan, meanwhile, was recognised in the Forbes 30 Under 30 Asia 2016 list in the enterprise technology category.[39] The annual list highlights the top 30 people below the age of 30 to watch in various industries in Asia. Three years later, she was one of 13 alumni conferred the NUS Outstanding Young Alumni Award.[40]

Like the people who inspired them during their NOC journey, Tiong and Guan want to pay it forward and help young entrepreneurs gain confidence to chase their dreams. Both return regularly to Singapore to share their start-up experience and give talks to NOC participants.

A change in mindset is overdue, said Guan.

     ❝ We should welcome a culture that says that as long as you dare to do something and work hard for it, you shouldn't be afraid to fail. ❞

CHAPTER 5

THE UNICORNS:
Carousell:
Mobile first
marketplace

(from left) Lucas Ngoo, Marcus Tan and Quek Siu Rui are three NOC alumni buddies who turned their idea of selling unwanted items into a multi-million dollar e-commerce business called Carousell.

"Dare to dream" is the mantra of Quek Siu Rui, Lucas Ngoo and Marcus Tan, the founders of one of Singapore's newest unicorns, Carousell. The online classifieds marketplace was established in 2012 and has since become a household name in Singapore, especially with its easy-to-navigate mobile-first app. In 2021, it was valued at US$1.1 billion, after raising US$100 million in its last round of funding led by South Korean private equity firm STIC Investments and another US$10 million from Singapore venture fund Heliconia.

Like the founders of PatSnap, the Carousell trio credited the NOC programme for inspiring them to be start-up entrepreneurs. For Quek, the company's chief executive, his epiphany came in 2011 when he went to work and study in Silicon Valley. **"Being there helped me to discover a passion for tech and solving problems that I otherwise would not have unlocked if I had gone ahead with a regular academic education."**

No less important was a failed attempt at building an app, which he and Ngoo, a fellow NOC intern and his housemate during the programme, attempted in 2011. While juggling classes and their internship jobs, they taught themselves how to code and the fundamentals of app building. The SoLoMo (social, local and mobile) marketing wave was also gaining momentum. Swept up by the tide of enthusiasm for this new marketing approach, they created a loyalty-based app for small, local businesses in Silicon Valley.

Called Sparkle, it would connect customers with businesses. For about six months, they worked on it every night after work and school, and throughout every weekend. A fish and chip shop eventually agreed to use it, but soon, it dawned on the duo that the owners were more intent on serving customers who came through the door than actively getting people to sign up for the app.

The experience also taught the budding entrepreneurs an important lesson, which would influence the way they approached their next venture. **"We weren't really invested in Sparkle. At the first instance of trouble, we began thinking of moving on to something else,"** said Quek. **"It didn't take off, but it taught us that we should create something that we genuinely cared about."**

When they returned home in 2012, the duo plunged into creating an app for people to sell their second-hand items easily. All a seller needed was a mobile phone to snap a picture of the product, a platform to upload it on and a buzzing marketplace to attract buyers.

The idea was triggered by the difficulty Quek faced when he tried to sell his tech gadgets such as a MacBook and cameras. He found the traditional online selling forums such as Yahoo! Auctions and HardwareZone tedious to navigate.

It also dawned on him that often, his smartphone, not his desktop, was his preferred device for emails, social media access and the selling of his gadgets. The 34-year-old said, **"Selling items on a forum through a desktop website was so painful. We searched the app store and there was nothing like what we wanted to do. We saw an opportunity to build it and make the experience a lot simpler."**

They named it Snapsell — the precursor to Carousell — and pitched it at Startup Weekend Singapore, an annual 54-hour hackathon that is now one of Southeast Asia's largest open innovation hackathons.

Along with the other hackathon teams, they had to convince the judges with just one line what their concept was about. The duo's winning line: "A dead simple way to sell your warez". After several selection rounds, peppered with moments of near-elimination, Team Snapsell was named the winner. The prize: a free three-month tenancy at BLOCK71.

Reflecting on the victorious moment in March 2012, Quek said:

❝❝ We had hundreds of people telling us that they wanted to know when we were launching. Some even asked if they could download the app right away. It was validation to do it full-time. ❞❞

Changing Tracks

Quek's move into the world of innovative tech was, like many NOC alumni, happenstance. Launching apps or becoming a technopreneur did not automatically feature on his career map when he started at NUS Business School in 2009. The general career path of most of his fellow undergraduates was to work in an investment bank, be a management consultant or brand manager.

He considered those pathways, but a conversation with Tan about the NOC programme piqued his curiosity about going to Silicon Valley and later, the alternative careers he could consider. Tan was his long-time friend from Ngee Ann Polytechnic's School of Business & Accountancy whom he met via a marketing interest group there.

Captivated by the possibility of studying and working in the US for a year, he applied for NOC when he entered NUS but was put on the waitlist. The following year he was given the nod to go to Silicon Valley, where he interned at video conference software company VSee. While attending classes at Stanford University, he got the chance to hear from guest lecturers such as Aaron Levie, co-founder and CEO of the enterprise cloud company Box, and Jack Dorsey, who co-founded microblogging and social networking service Twitter as well as financial services and digital payments company Block.

The internship experience was invaluable, he said:

❝ Because VSee's resources were finite, we were entrusted to do a full-timer's job. I did everything, from customer support to marketing and product management, and I saw how hands-on the founder and the members of the first team were. ❞

This "formative experience" from the NOC programme also put him and his Carousell partners on a quest to build something for the greater good. Additionally, their individual experiences at various start-ups made them want to run their business in a way that will **"empower our teammates and build a Mission First culture with a flat hierarchy"**.

The entrepreneurs they had met in Silicon Valley and the tech giants they had listened to instilled in them the value of putting users first and solving problems, instead of just chasing profits.

Quek said:

> " The idea is to solve problems, build great products and services and make a meaningful impact on many people. Financial outcomes would be by-products. "

In short, do not just chase profits, he added.

Quek also attended a Startup School event organised by Y Combinator, the famed American company that provides seed funding for start-ups and helps them develop their ideas. He had close encounters as well with tech luminaries such as Meta's Mark Zuckerberg and actor Ashton Kutcher, who is an active Silicon Valley investor. These were "life-changing" moments, he added. **"Hearing them tell their stories made me realise that they were no different from me when they started. In some cases, they had no work experience, but they were all on a mission to solve problems for people even though they had limited resources."**

No Looking Back

Things moved quickly post-hackathon. A month later, Quek and Ngoo tried but failed to win a S$10,000 Venture Ideation Grant from NUS Enterprise. They made another attempt and literally did an elevator pitch to Prof Wong Poh Kam, who was then the director of the NUS Entrepreneurship Centre and Academic Advisor for the NOC programme. He was convinced. A day later, they received word that they would be given S$7,000 to further develop their idea.

Meanwhile, Tan, who has a business administration degree from NUS, quit his job as a business development consultant at computer technology giant Oracle and joined them as the third co-founder, taking charge of the app's interface design. Quek, who made it twice to the Dean's List and received the NUS Global Merit Scholarship and NUS Overseas College (Silicon Valley) Scholarship, opted out of doing his honours degree and focused on product development. **"In creating a start-up, I was doing my honours in the school of hard knocks,"** he said with a grin.

Ngoo, who was completing his last semester for a computer engineering degree, juggled schoolwork and coding for the app. The 34-year-old recalled:

66 On weekdays, I would spend the day attending classes in school, and head over to BLOCK71 in the evening to code. On weekends, the three of us would work on the app from morning till we had to get the last train home. It was exciting because we were creating a mobile-first way for people to buy and sell things and, in turn, could make an impact on people's lives with technology. 99

By May 2012, the trio was fully immersed in start-up life. Quek took charge of product management while Tan, 37, took care of the app's interface design. Ngoo did the coding for the app and backend work.

Along the way, they also changed the app's name from Snapsell to Carousell, inspired by the Kodak Carousel Projector on the television drama *Mad Men*. The way they saw it: Each listing on Carousell resembled a slide film that gets projected into a marketplace, with each item going round and round from person to person. **"We wanted it to be fun like a merry-go-round carousel and added an extra L to reflect the core utility of 'sell',"** Quek said.

The High and The Low

On 13 August 2012, the Carousell app went live. Quek called it the proudest moment of his start-up life. **"Our idea became an actual product. After we pressed the button to release the app, we raised a toast to ourselves with beer we bought from Cold Storage supermarket."** By the third day of Carousell's launch, the app was ranked second among the Top Free Lifestyle Apps in Singapore on Apple's App Store.

The euphoria, however, was brief, as they witnessed the daily sign-ups dwindling to fewer than 10 three months later. The buzzing digital marketplace they had envisioned did not materialise.

Undeterred, they tapped on existing users' data and continued to ask new sign-ups about how they interacted with the app. The information they gathered showed that females between 15 and 24 years of age were the most active users, selling and buying mostly fashion items and beauty products.

Armed with the information, they went to flea markets and met blogshop retailers and sellers of pre-loved clothes. As Carousell's community managers, Quek and Tan reached out to women's magazines and wrote their own articles for the app such as "Top Five

Peplum Tops" and "Top Five LBDs (little black dresses) to Have" to push eyeballs to sellers. Though they were out of their depth, they persisted, confident that their product was a winner.

Quek found comfort in the words of Paul Graham, co-founder of Y Combinator and a prolific investor, who had said:

> **It's better to have 100 people that love you than a million people that just sort of like you. Find 100 people that love you.**

Being at BLOCK71 also helped them stay the course. Surrounded by other innovators and start-ups, the Carousell co-founders would often pop into their offices to seek advice and get energised to keep going. Another inspiring presence was Darius Cheung, an NOC alumni with whom they shared a space.

Finding Momentum and Hitting Their Stride

Soon, the Carousell trio found their groove.

In January 2013, Carousell received a S$50,000 ACE Startups Grant and was incorporated as a company. By November 2013, they raised S$1 million in seed funding from venture capital groups that included Japan-based Rakuten Ventures and 500 Global headquartered in San Francisco. Individuals like Cheung also came on board as angel investors.

A year later, the company was ranked the top shopping app in Singapore on Apple's App Store and growing fast. It was a sweet payoff for the co-founders who had gone a year-and-a-half with no pay and living frugally on their savings. They never took a cab, travelled only on buses and trains, and ate cheap hawker food.

Though the schedule to build their company was punishing, the trio did give themselves small indulgences. They made time to have meals with their families once a week. To celebrate a newcomer or a teammate's birthday, they would take a night off to have a meal at Wala Wala in Holland Village or food park Timbre+ near their office, where they would catch their favourite local band 53A perform. When restlessness or mental blocks hit at night, they would take a short break by playing Counter-Strike, the popular multiplayer first-person shooter video game.

Their hard work and commitment to their dream paid off grandly, with the 2021 announcement that Carousell had become a unicorn.

The start-up currently has more than 700 employees across Southeast Asia, as well as Taiwan and Hong Kong. It has also evolved into a thriving marketplace beyond just users hawking used goods. Today, new cars, luxury watches and even real estate can be transacted on the portal.

In 2019, Carousell merged with 701Search, the classifieds firm owned by Norwegian telco Telenor Group, and took over three of 701Search's online marketplaces — Mudah, Malaysia; Cho Tot, Vietnam, and OneKyat, Myanmar. It has also expanded, under its own brand name, to eight other markets, including Indonesia, Hong Kong, Taiwan, Malaysia and the Philippines.

Its burgeoning clout has attracted top talents such as JJ Eastwood, the former managing director for Asia-Pacific at Rakuten Marketing, who is the managing director of Carousell Media Group and Igor Volynskiy, the former technology executive vice president of Lazada Group who is its chief technology officer. A recent addition is former Razer Executive Edwin Chan, who is the chief financial officer.

Despite Carousell's success and media exposure, the trio's initial mission remains paramount, said Quek. **"We feel a deep sense of responsibility because we are one of the early players in Singapore's Internet start-up space. We know people are watching our progress, but we continue to keep our heads down and focus on our mission."**

That mission, as he defines it, is to inspire the world to start selling their underutilised items, and eventually, second-hand goods will become the first choice for people and this will be a victory for the environment. **"The pandemic has shown us that our mission... is more relevant than ever,"** Quek shared in an interview with *The Straits Times* after news of the company's new unicorn status was announced. Beyond that, he notes the portal has evolved into helping people have side hustles or even make ends meet with the products they sell, without the intervention of middlemen.

He quotes the Dalai Lama, who said, **"A meaningful life isn't about acquiring money and other facilities; it's about dedicating your life to helping others as much as you can."** This principle has guided the trio in growing their business, including choosing who to work with and not just focusing on the amount of money an investor brings to the table.

He added:

> ❝ One thing we took away from the NOC programme was to use technology to solve problems and make an impact on the world. That was always the goal. It's a big mission, but we just take it step-by-step and keep improving day by day. ❞

CHAPTER 6

THE E-COMMERCE LEADER:
Chris Feng

Chris Feng, an NOC alumni, joined Sea originally to manage its mobile gaming business before being appointed CEO of Shopee, where he grew the e-commerce platform to be one of the largest in Southeast Asia. He is Group President of Sea, Shopee's parent company.

When online marketplace Shopee burst onto the Southeast Asian e-commerce scene in 2015,[41] it faced at least four regional rivals: Lazada, Zalora, Qoo10 and Tokopedia. The oldest was Tokopedia, born in 2009, and the youngest, then regional leader Lazada, at three years old.

Today, some seven years later, the Johnny-come-lately is a juggernaut,[42] topping the Southeast Asian list of e-commerce platforms with the most visits. It ranks first in the Shopping category in both Southeast Asia and Taiwan by average monthly active users, total time spent in app on Android as well as downloads for the year 2020, according to analytics firm App Annie.

Driving the explosive growth is Chris Feng[43] and his leadership team who have helmed the business from the start. He joined Shopee's parent company Sea (then known as Garena) in March 2014 to head its mobile game business. By July 2015, he was named Chief Executive Officer (CEO) of newly-formed Shopee by the Singapore-based technology group and in March 2020, took on the role of CEO at SeaMoney, the digital payment and financial services unit of the company. In January 2022, Feng became Sea's Group President.

As Shopee's chief executive, Feng has grown the platform and led the charge beyond the shores of Singapore into about 15 markets across Asia,[44] South America and Europe. After the initial launch in Singapore, Malaysia, Thailand, Indonesia, Vietnam, the Philippines and Taiwan, it took a giant leap from its home region into South America in 2019. Brazil was the first stop and in two years, Shopee shot up to the No.1 spot in the Shopping category by downloads and total time spent in app, according to App Annie.

Despite the Covid-19 pandemic, Shopee continues to find opportunities to connect buyers and sellers. It had expanded to South America. However, in September 2022, it shut operations in Argentina, Chile, Columbia and Mexico due to economic uncertainty. Its operations in Brazil are unaffected.

Fuelling the company's growth is not only the pandemic which has led to an e-commerce boom as people are sheltered at home, but also its focus on adapting to the specific local needs of the various economies, most notably the growing number of mobile users. Shopee is one of the leading pioneers in the region that created a mobile-first, instead of a web-based, marketplace where consumers can browse, shop and sell easily through their mobile phones.

Coupled with the ease of tracking delivery and integrated payments that includes its own mobile wallet ShopeePay, the Singapore company is among the region's leading e-commerce platform with a global presence.

The journey, however, has its fair share of ups and downs, says Feng in an email interview. He also describes how the NOC programme has shaped his dream to be an entrepreneur, explains some of the challenges the company faced along the way and what's in store next at Shopee.

You spent one year in Silicon Valley as an NOC Intern, working in a start-up and studying at Stanford University under its Management Science programme. What is one lesson that has had a lifelong impact and helped you build and expand Shopee, especially in the face of the Covid-19 pandemic?

One thing I discovered at NOC is that what makes you uncomfortable can also be your biggest opportunity for growth and impact. Life is unpredictable. There are many ups and downs. In business, the factors impacting us can change very quickly. When we face challenges, I feel the best thing we can do is to make the most of what life presents.

Take the pandemic for example. When it first struck, things changed almost overnight for everyone. It was not easy. We had to deal with a lot of uncertainties, just as the world did. I recall having multiple discussions with our teams every day. We had to make critical and practical decisions, while faced with rapid changes that were not in our control.

But we saw buyers relying on our platform for access to essential goods. Sellers needed to go online to sell their products and survive. We found ourselves in a position to make an impact in the region. So, we chose to adapt quickly, work even harder and help our communities overcome the challenges.

We accepted what we could not change and focused on what we needed to do to make an impact.

2

Other lessons that you continue to cherish?

I can share a couple of other lessons. One is on big picture thinking.

I was fortunate to have met the most talented tech entrepreneurs and the best minds in Silicon Valley through my NOC experience. I observed that many of these successful people have a deep understanding of the bigger picture as well as being able to navigate short-term issues. It's like being a satellite — having both a clear view of the entire earth and being able to zoom into key areas when needed.

That impacted how I think about leadership. I often encourage our leaders at Shopee to consider the bigger picture. To think about whether we are creating value for the longer term. Do we make lives better? Are we doing the right things for our communities, our customers, our people? Let me give an example. When Shopee started, we knew we couldn't stop at just helping more sellers come on board. We needed to help them learn, adapt and grow their business.

So, we set up Shopee University to help our sellers develop business skills. I'm glad to see that many of them are keen learners. Beyond that, they are keen to spread their knowledge too, sharing tips and teaching others. Now, we have a lively community of sellers who support each other and help even more businesses benefit from e-commerce.

Another lesson I learnt was coaching and feedback.

During my internship, I got the opportunity to learn about business and coaching from one of the best coaches in Silicon Valley. The course was not just about how to coach others, but how to be coached. One memorable piece of advice he gave was that any feedback received is a chance to learn. Especially the tough ones. Even if the feedback itself is known to you already, or is something you disagree with, you can still take the opportunity to learn what others think about your behaviour and to know the person's thinking process better.

This shaped the way I think about our culture at Shopee. For us, it's important that we build a strong feedback culture. We have taken many tangible steps such as building a feedback system and starting group feedback sessions to encourage all team members to give and receive feedback.

I often encourage team members to send their feedback directly to me as well. Because of that, I've been better able to understand many of their real concerns and act on some matters that they care about. We still have a long way to go in building a culture wherein team members openly share direct feedback with me. But I feel we are moving in the right direction.

Finally, I learnt an interesting lesson from one of the classes at Stanford on decision-making. It was about the probability of decisions. In each multiple choice question, we had to give each answer a probability of being correct, rather than choosing one correct answer. For some questions, I was so confident my answer was correct I put a 100 per cent probability. But I was wrong. I thought I would definitely fail the class. Thankfully, I found out later that it was just a small test and didn't count towards our final result.

That taught me a valuable lesson — nothing is impossible. In my career, I have found myself reflecting on this lesson often when making decisions.

What inspired the name Shopee?

There was no complex thinking process behind it. When we came up with it, we simply felt it was simple and related to the word "Shopping". We wanted a name that could be easily recognised by people of diverse backgrounds, and hopefully one that made people happy when they heard it. That was it. For me, keeping things simple has always been key.

Can you describe the major struggles in the initial days?

It was just a few years ago, in 2015, when we were a small team sharing a corner space in Murray Terrace in Chinatown.

When we started, no one had heard of us and no one wanted to work with us. It wasn't easy finding partners. There were already other well-established players on the scene, and there were people sceptical of the e-commerce market as well.

We decided to focus on listening to our sellers to understand what they needed. They told us about their frustrations and the ways the existing players did not serve them. We then worked on designing our platform to make selling more convenient and help them be more successful in selling online.

We also started with very few resources — not even a product to show potential sellers because we had set ourselves a target to acquire 500 sellers in three months before launching the app in May 2015. We completed the website just before the launch date, so before that we had nothing concrete to show sellers even as we were trying to convince them to come on board.

On top of that, we started off with a system that was much more basic than what we have now. Many things had to be done manually. The team had to upload the first 10,000 stock-keeping units (SKUs) line by line. All the products had to be listed on our app one at a time.

I guess we saw ourselves as a group of underdogs with a strong survival spirit. More than just looking at the struggles as challenges, we wanted to make the impossible possible. And when faced with tough obstacles, we fought as if our lives depended on it.

It's a spirit we never want to forget. We will never settle. We will always have the mentality that we could lose all our successes tomorrow. I feel that drives us and defines our leadership team.

What have been Shopee's top achievements so far? Which achievements are you most proud of? Why?

I'm proud of our team and the hard work they have consistently put in to support businesses, communities and shoppers.

They are a key reason we've achieved many milestones. For example, we grew from humble beginnings to currently having offices in more than 20 cities around the world. We were also one of the pioneers to recognise the potential of mobile in our region. In 2016, we launched the first 9.9 Mobile Shopping Day, when people can enjoy significant discounts. Now it's called 9.9 Super Shopping Day and has become one of the biggest events during the year-end festive season.

On a personal level, what makes me feel most satisfied is how we can make a difference in people's lives. I remember in a class on Global Entrepreneurial Marketing at Stanford, we had a guest speaker who shared why he started his company. I'm paraphrasing, but it went something like, "One day, when you're gone, how many people will think that the world is better because of you or something you had contributed?"

This has stuck with me. In the Shopee context, I'm happy that we have been able to better the lives of small local business owners, especially those who were struggling to make the leap into online retail. In this way, I feel that we have impacted a group of people who might have been left behind.

Take our seller Maria, for example. When she started her bedsheet business in Indonesia in 2008, she did everything by hand. To promote her business, she went door-to-door to distribute brochures to her neighbours. It was painstaking work, and her business grew slowly over eight years as it was focused mainly on local customers. She then took the advice of another seller and set up a shop on Shopee, which opened a whole new market to her. She now sells hundreds of locally-made sheets every day to customers all over Southeast Asia. Her success has also benefited others in her community as she currently employs 20 people, including many who dropped out of school.

How has the NOC programme influenced your entrepreneurial journey?

What helped the most was my exposure to some of the best minds in the world and that gave me insights into how they think. My internship allowed me to learn first-hand how start-ups run and how the founders made decisions. Those insights helped me when I found myself leading a start-up.

Even though I was only an intern then, the Chief Technology Officer (CTO) of the company assigned me to be a core member of the product & development team as well as be involved in the end-to-end delivery cycle. He also spent a lot of time coaching and advising me. The impact his humility and leadership had on people and the business stayed with me in my entrepreneurial journey.

Also, living in another country exposed me to a variety of ways of working and thinking because the students on the programme came from different countries in the world. Discussions with them made me realise that diversity is a strength. Because our points of view were so different, we explored ideas further than if we had all come from the same place.

I'm happy to see that at Shopee, our teams are becoming more diverse, with frequent collaboration among different offices and countries. One way we are encouraging this is to make English the official common language and provide regular programmes to help those who need to improve. At the same time, we also have courses for other languages, so those who wish to better connect with their peers in the local language can do so. For example, I have been learning Bahasa Indonesia for the past few years. Though I'm far from fluent, I enjoy being able to use it sometimes when talking to Indonesian team members, as well as our buyers and sellers.

Finally, NOC was great for meeting people and networking. I was part of NOC student associations as well as the core committees of a few associations at Stanford University. Through these connections, I made many great friends. I learnt a lot from them, and some even became business partners.

What is the one piece of advice you would give a young person setting out to be an entrepreneur?

Be ready to seize opportunities, even ones you didn't expect.

I did not know about NOC until quite late. One of my friends, who wanted to join the programme, asked for my opinion on it and whether I would be interested in joining as well. I saw it was a good opportunity and signed up.

In life and business, the ability to identify opportunities and move quickly will open many doors for you. Don't be afraid to step out of your comfort zone. As I mentioned at the beginning, the things that make you uncomfortable can be your biggest opportunities for impact and growth. When these opportunities come calling, have the courage to respond positively.

How has e-commerce in the region changed since Shopee appeared on the scene?

E-commerce has grown significantly, especially during the pandemic. Consumers today expect more than a transactional experience. From discovering new products, being entertained, to receiving their deliveries quickly, it now needs to be even more seamless.

Businesses, too, have adopted a digital-first mindset. They will keep pushing the boundaries of the online experience.

While e-commerce is much more common today, it is only a fraction of the retail market. There is still work to be done. We need to enable even more users to come online, to be part of the region's digital economy.

What's next for Shopee?

We are still at the start of our journey. There's so much more that we can do to create a more inclusive ecosystem in all our markets. We're very grateful for the support we've received. We want to ensure that we can continue to positively impact our local communities.

CHAPTER 7

THE INFLUENCERS I:
Serial Entrepreneur Darius Cheung

Darius Cheung in November 2010.

With his list of achievements, Darius Cheung is often dubbed a multi-hyphenate: poster boy of the NUS Overseas Colleges (NOC) programme/angel investor/serial entrepreneur/mentor and, more recently, co-founder of Southeast Asia's fastest-growing property portal — 99.co.

But the 41-year-old is quick to point out, with a laugh, that his first venture into commerce did not end well. He lost money. His inventory was confiscated and his teacher, to put it mildly, was not amused. **"However, I picked up some invaluable and enduring lessons,"** he said of his teen years' attempt to make some extra pocket money. **"One big lesson is that the new business must be a service or product that people want and need."**

An only child, Cheung had been plucked out of school in Hong Kong at age 13 and sent to Singapore in 1996 to continue his studies. His China-born parents, who run their own small printing business in Hong Kong, paid his school fees and accommodation at Hwa Chong Institution and gave him enough for the bare essentials, such as stationery and books. **"Anything else, like video games, were luxuries and I had to find the means to pay for them or do without."**

A keen fan of VCD movies, he saw the moneymaking potential and sank his business milk teeth into trading. He brought VCDs from Hong Kong that were unavailable in Singapore and sold them to his schoolmates. Business was brisk. **"In a month, I sold out the first lot of VCDs, earning me enough to buy my first CD-ROM recorder and put aside some as savings."**

He paid S$400, his entire year's profits from the VCD sales, to buy the device and made copies of CDs for sale. But his joy was short-lived. The school's discipline master found out, confiscated the 14-year-old's recorder and VCD inventory, and shut down his business.

66 The experience was good though. I learnt the heavy cost of holding too much inventory, the need to maintain a lean operation and the importance of having savings for tough times. Financial grit is paramount in business. 99

Enterprise and self-reliance were obviously in his genes. His parents had, in the late 1960s, moved to then British-governed Hong Kong to escape the political turmoil of the Cultural Revolution that engulfed China in the 1970s. Then the 1997 handover of Hong Kong to China drew near, political uncertainty haunted them again. Cheung's parents believed he would have a better life in Singapore.

"You could say they are farsighted," Cheung said with pride.

He has since made his parents proud as well. A graduate in electrical and computer engineering from the National University of Singapore (NUS), Darius is the poster boy of the NOC programme, following his success with tenCube. He had co-founded the start-up, which secures mobile phones in 2005 with Varun Chatterji, an NOC alumni, and Rishi Israni, an NUS student. In 2010, they made waves internationally when McAfee acquired it for a confidential eight-figure sum.

With his new millions and much-talked-about achievement, Cheung was sought after to be advisor, mentor and angel investor to the next generation of entrepreneurial NOC alumni. Among them were Quek Siu Rui, co-founder of online marketplace Carousell, and Royston Tay, co-founder of Zopim which provides real-time chat widgets for websites.

Like tenCube, Zopim was also acquired by an American company, Zendesk. The San Francisco-based customer service company paid US$30 million in 2014 for the seven-year-old company. The purchase reportedly would grant each of its four co-founders more than US$10 million in cash and stock options after a three-year period.

Cheung was bitten by the start-up bug again. And again, the idea stemmed from a personal problem. With tenCube, a co-founder had lost his phone and was troubled by not only the loss of personal information but also strangers getting hold of the data. This time, it was Cheung being bugged by a tedious task. Like many young adults, he was co-living in an apartment and tracking shared expenses was a monthly headache. The chore sparked the creation of a bill-sharing app in 2012, three years after tenCube's acquisition. Named Billpin, it received S$50,000 seed funding from a government scheme called i.JAM.[45] Cheung considers Billpin a failed project because it did not catch on. He shut it down.

Along the way, the Billpin team of about six people uncovered another common issue: finding the right flatmates. It prompted the creation of Homie, a flatmate-finding app, in 2014. In the process, Cheung and his team formed 99.co, a map-based property search portal, to address the bigger problem of finding the right neighbourhood with the relevant amenities, such as food options and proximity to the Mass Rapid Transport (MRT) train system.

In all his ventures, Cheung said, he is driven by one a major motivation: a desire to improve lives to pay back to the community that helped him succeed.

In the Beginning

No less important in Cheung's tech success is his discovery of the Internet in the late 1990s, while studying at Hwa Chong Junior College. Yahoo! opened new worlds to him. For email, he had a Hotmail address. For chats, he used ICQ ("I Seek You"), an early form of instant messaging. To dive into issues, he signed up for Internet Relay Chat (IRC) to get into discussion forums.

These tools also aroused his curiosity about their inventors. **"I discovered they were developed by a few guys in a place called Silicon Valley. I was awed and promised myself to get to Silicon Valley one day."**

He did not have to wait long. While a second-year student in electrical and computer engineering at NUS he discovered the NOC programme.

Silicon Valley now seemed within reach. To demonstrate his interest in entrepreneurship, he joined the NUS Entrepreneurship Society, and attended its networking sessions and start-up events. He also formed a team to enter a business plan competition: The idea was to create a virtual expo that would complement Singapore's exhibition and conference sector. They reached the semi-finals.

It was enough to overcome the stiff competition from a large pool of NOC wannabes and in January 2003, he flew into San Francisco as a member of the third batch of NOC interns. Actuate, a Nasdaq-listed enterprise software company, took him in as a marketing assistant and his duties included producing various reports and sending e-mailers to potential customers. Twice a week, he would attend technopreneurship courses at Stanford University.

"It was my first exposure to digital marketing and as a geek, I lapped it up but within three months, I was bored. It had nothing to do with Actuate, however." As a listed company, its job roles were more specific. Cheung had only marketing activities on his plate, unlike NOC interns at smaller start-ups who had to do a variety of tasks.

With time on his hands, he joined and became President of the NOC Student Association in Silicon Valley. He organised meetups and networking sessions with entrepreneurs and investors, as well as forums on topics of interest to the interns, such as Singapore's role in start-up development and the types of activities for building a start-up community.

His experiences and encounters during the 12-month stint gave him two insights that made him more confident:

" One, it's not necessary to ask for permission to do something different and the other is that everyone is a human being, regardless of his or her success in Silicon Valley. What differentiates the Silicon Valley high achievers from us is their sense of purpose, some luck, the opportunity to do something and then deciding they could do it. In short, they are people who persist in making their dreams come true. **"**

The realisation enabled him to breach the psychological threshold that entrepreneurial success is dependent on hard skills, like coding.

Hence, Jerry Yang, co-founder of Yahoo!, is still his hero but is no longer placed on a pedestal, he said with a smile, adding: **"In Singapore, people grow up in a society where it's not always a given that you can try and do new things. In Silicon Valley, people who break the rules are celebrated."**

The First Start-up

Cheung's new-found confidence led him to start a business on his return to Singapore although the self-confessed geek blithely admits that he does not have the charisma of famous entrepreneurs like Apple's late founder Steve Jobs.

His Silicon Valley housemates, Chatterji and Israni, were also as psyched up to launch their own tech start-ups. The trio pooled their US$30,000 savings and, with the support of the NUS' School of Computing, his housemates' alma mater, opened an office in an old and unused lecture room in 2005. It was rent-free.

As they tinkered with various ideas, Chatterjji lost his expensive mobile phone, a misfortune that subsequently became a stroke of serendipity. His Nokia 6610 mobile phone was one of the earliest megapixel phones with colour and was able to run software on it.

But like mobile devices then, his phone had no tracking software which would have enabled its data to be remotely wiped out and the phone turned off. Such a feature would render the phone useless and allow the owner to protect his or her information.

The need for such a software was obvious but after developing it, they struggled to sell it to consumers as there were no app store and payment gateway. Buyers had to download the software from tenCube's website onto their computer and then to their mobile phone. When installed, buyers had to refer to tenCube's website for an activation key to turn on the software.

"We had just five customers. The process was too complicated," Cheung acknowledged.

tenCube founders (from left) Rishi Israna, Varun Chatterji, Indradeep Biswas and Darius Cheung share a light-hearted moment in their Singapore Science Park office.

Selling through the telcos was a possibility, except that mobile phones were still a rarity, making up only five per cent of the market in 2006. Worse, the telco would take the bulk of the revenue, leaving tenCube with only 30 per cent.

As they worked feverishly on a solution, a new demand emerged. Some police officers were taking photos of crime scenes with their personal mobile phones and transmitting the information back to their office. Operationally, this made sense. But should the phone be lost, the information would be gone, too.

The Singapore Police Force needed to digitally secure the mobile phones so that when lost, the phone could be locked remotely, and the information erased. tenCube was awarded the contract to develop it because Chatterji was the sole developer in Singapore who could write the security software in Symbian, the operating system of Nokia handphones which dominated the mobile market then.

With the S$70,000 deal, tenCube hired about 10 to 15 software developers whose work helped build the start-up's deep knowledge and experience in mobile security.

"Do you know that if the information was deleted from the recycle bin in the handphone, the data can still be recovered? The correct way to delete data is to rewrite over it seven times to leave no trace of it," Cheung explained. **"We had to produce this data wiping software in a few months."** They did.

It was followed by a steady flow of business from government organisations, such as the Defence Science and Technology Agency and other security-related agencies.

When the iPhone arrived in 2007, the smartphone market took off and in no time, it made up about one-third of the business of Singapore's telcos. Consumers were able to receive email on their phones and willingly paid monthly subscriptions to secure their data. The telcos circled back to tenCube to seek security features to protect mobile emails. tenCube's business boomed.

Smartphone vendors such as Sony Ericsson and Nokia, the two major players then, became tenCube's customers as well. They bundled the security features into their phones and paid tenCube S$1.50 for each device sold.

tenCube next developed a mobile security software called WaveSecure, an invention that led McAfee to buy the company in 2010.

Selling tenCube was a tough decision for Cheung and his fellow co-founders. **"It was our baby — and was profitable,"** he said, adding that it could have grown bigger, which would have boosted its valuation and, in turn, the selling price.

NOC, however, was reaching its 10th Anniversary in 2012. tenCube's exit would be a strong testimony to the success of the NUS experiment in nurturing entrepreneurship. It would also encourage the hundreds of NOC alumni, who had founded their own start-ups, to press on.

"We took our win for the greater good of the start-up community. It's not about us, but the whole Singapore tech start-up environment. It would give them a lot of encouragement," said Cheung.

The acquisition made the trio, who were no more than 30 years old, multimillionaires. The sale price remains under wraps, although observers had speculated that it was between S$15 million and S$25 million.

Competing with a Gorilla

After fulfilling a transition commitment at McAfee, Cheung soon took the plunge again and launched his next big thing in 2014: online property platform 99.co. The name underpins the desire of the three founders — Cheung, Conor McLaughlin and Yan Phun — to serve the 99 per cent of people who are unserved or underserved in the property market.

Their need became obvious when the subprime crisis in the US thrashed the global financial market between 2007 and 2010, hitting homeowners hard, including the majority in Singapore.

It triggered the idea of a real estate service that was transparent and intuitive. Keen investors trooped in. In 2014, 99.co raised US$560,000 in seed funding from investors like Golden Gate Ventures. The following year, with Facebook co-founder Eduardo Saverin as the lead investor, 99.co raised US$1.6 million. Six years later, Saverin, who is based in Singapore, would pump in more money. He declined to disclose the sum but said that he was drawn by Cheung's desire to improve people's lives by making house-hunting more convenient. **"He's not out to create a disruption or get a return on investment,"** Saverin added. Cheung himself had poured in hundreds of thousands of dollars, making it his largest investment in a start-up to date.

Incumbent PropertyGuru, however, was not indifferent to the newcomer's appearance. Founded in 2007, it dominates the Southeast Asian market, with about 57,000 partner property agents and 3.3 million available housing options monthly. In 2020, its revenue was S$82.1 million.

To compete, Cheung focused on creating a real estate listing with algorithms that allow home renters, buyers, sellers and property agents to do their search swiftly and efficiently. One of 99.co's major features is the ranking of rental and sale listings according to complete and timely information, and not by the fees paid to it by property agents or owners.

The business model favours posts with lots of photographs that give a good picture of the property's significant features, and useful information such as commuting times to business districts, proximity to schools and local dining options.

Another key difference is that property listers pay it a fee only when a house-hunter makes an inquiry, a feature that encourages sellers and agents to improve the appeal of their listings.

Still, PropertyGuru is the 800-pound Gorilla. Its 2020 revenue was S$82.1 million compared to 99.co's US$5.5 million. But for 99.co, its revenue was a 62 per cent jump over the US$3.4 million it reported in 2019. This makes the company the fastest-growing property portal in Southeast Asia, the Covid-19 pandemic notwithstanding. Fuelling its growth was an increase in subscriptions, business partnerships and package offerings like virtual viewings, as well as cost-cutting measures that included Cheung foregoing his salary for about nine months.

The rivalry led to a legal suit in 2015 when PropertyGuru sued 99.co for copyright infringement. It involved 99.co's mobile app named Xpressor, which lets property agents cross-post their listings with the photographs showing the PropertyGuru watermark. But the Singapore High Court dismissed PropertyGuru's claims that 99.co had infringed its copyright by reproducing photos with the PropertyGuru watermark.

Justice Hoo Sheau Peng said: "The addition of the watermark does not, in my judgment, make the altered image an original work". PropertyGuru was ordered to pay 40 per cent of the legal costs. Justice Hoo, however, also concluded that a 2015 settlement agreement between both parties was breached by 99.co which reproduced substantial content from its rival.

Rising above Covid-19

The pandemic-induced restrictions on movement did not dent the company's business. On the contrary, it grew. Monthly traffic across its three sites — 99.co, Rumah123 and iProperty.com.sg — jumped 52 per cent, from 13 million visits in February 2020 to 19.8 million in June 2020. Revenue also rose by 60 per cent in 2020.

The pandemic curbs also raised 99.co's profile and reputation as property transactions were increasingly compelled to go online since in-person viewings were restricted, if not impossible.

It received US$33 million in funding, which has allowed it to expand into Indonesia where it acquired property portal Rumah123.com. In Singapore it acquired iProperty.com.sg and SRX.

New Features to Stop Discrimination

As with his first start-up tenCube, Cheung recounted how a personal experience again got the founders to address a disturbing problem.

In 2015, he had gone in search of an apartment near the office of his pregnant wife Roshni Mahtani, so that she could minimise time on the road. Although many were available, landlords would, on discovering that his wife is Indian, declare that the apartments were not available.

Unsettled by the overt racial discrimination, Cheung launched the Regardless of Race campaign on 99.co to curb such exclusion in the Singapore property market. He also included a Diversity Friendly listing option for landlords and real estate agents. The tag indicates all are welcome regardless of race, ethnicity, religion, age, gender identity, sexual orientation or physical disability.

These features dovetail aptly with Cheung's business vision to use his companies as a platform to create a better world.

Yet another timely move amid Covid-19 was the introduction of video listing that property agents can use to take potential buyers on a virtual tour of homes for sale. To coax more agents to use it, 99.co held online tutorials. As a result, about 25 per cent of its agents now use the feature, a rise from five per cent in 2018 when it was introduced.

These measures required Cheung to beef up the company's tech arsenal. About 100 technologists were to be hired between 2021 and 2022 for its team in Singapore and Indonesia.

Looking ahead, he envisioned more new products that will, among other things, help tackle the issue of rising property prices, which is putting home ownership out of reach of many young adults in Southeast Asia.

Covid-19 may have delayed the introduction of property-related financial products, but Cheung is optimistic.

"Look out for new features and solutions in the near future," he declared with a grin.

CHAPTER 8

THE INFLUENCERS II:
Start-up trailblazer
Goh Yi Ping

The go-getter Goh Yi Ping believed the entrepreneurship experience she gained during the NOC programme was useful in founding start-ups and working in organisations.

The prime mover in technopreneur and venture capitalist Goh Yiping's eventful life is handily captured in a quartet of abbreviations: NUS, NOC, SARS and US.

NUS is the country's oldest university and, for many decades, its only university, where Goh studied for a bachelor's degree in real estate management. NOC is the entrepreneurship development programme that propelled her from college student to trainee entrepreneur in 2003. That was the year the outbreak of the deadly Severe Acute Respiratory Syndrome, or SARS for short, derailed her plans for an internship in China, flipping her trajectory across the Pacific to the US. The rest, as some might say, is yet another enduring chapter of Singapore's entrepreneurial history in the making.

But let's not get ahead of the big story, the genesis of the life-changing opportunity that is the NOC.

When Goh signed up for her 2003 NOC internship, she was part of only the second cohort of students to try out this new technopreneurship experiment. Today, two decades later, she gives it high marks for the immeasurable support it provided and continues to provide fledgling entrepreneurs. With the perspective of time and several start-ups under her belt, and now as a start-up ecosystem developer, this is how she summed up the value of the programme:

> **The NOC widened my perspective, so I found it easy to finish my degree; it didn't take a lot for me to do well in real estate. Somehow, NOC made me more efficient and open-minded. In Year 4, I did well and made the Dean's List.**

But at the start, she had to deal with a setback. She recalled her inauspicious introduction to NOC: **"I was supposed to go to Shanghai, was super keen to go and wanted to learn about doing business from the Chinese. I thought 'if I can survive China, I can survive anywhere'."**

"Then SARS happened."

The deadly viral outbreak torpedoed her intended stint in Shanghai, and NOC offered her the chance to go to Philadelphia instead:

> ❝ I was one of the earliest [of the NOC interns] to arrive in Philly. It was May 2003 and I stayed till late August 2004. I was then working towards a Bachelor of Science (Real Estate) degree and didn't have tech experience. I wanted to find out what it meant to be in the tech business. It was pre-iPhone and pre-Facebook days; it was still Friendster then. Google was about to gain momentum. In Philadelphia, I saw a whole new way of learning. I learnt how to fundraise, pitch well and gain domain knowledge quickly. It was a steep learning curve. Not knowing didn't mean I can't do it. ❞

After several interviews, two companies accepted her: media company Nroute Communications and Osiris Communications, a branding, marketing and research company. They, however, wanted her for roles that were less tech and more about business development and project management. She chose Nroute but ended up interning at both.

Nroute's media streaming content was shown on buses and trains that travelled interstate.

   ❝ I learnt a lot, from media editing to business development to sales. There were up to eight of us in the full-time team, including another NOC intern. I was making US$700 a month and most of the time they couldn't pay me. It got difficult for them, so I left and joined Osiris. But I continued helping Nroute part-time. **❞**

At Osiris, she worked more on research and branding.

The interns' schedule was punishing. The start-ups were required to give them time off once or twice a week to attend classes. Said Goh, who was studying at the University of Pennsylvania (UPenn):

   ❝ We study in the daytime and do project work at night. There was a lot of juggling. I thought that as I was in my 20s, I should push myself, then I can choose what I want to do when I'm older. **❞**

And push herself she did. **"I slept four hours on average, managing 1.5 companies and essentially working for free for Nroute."**

   ❝ Money was tight. Coming from a lower middle-income family, there were no extras for me. For the first few months, I scrimped and saved to survive on US$700 a month. But NOC was helpful, topping up my monthly pay to US$1,000. My mum had to borrow a few thousand dollars to tide me over. But the loans were quickly repaid once I graduated and started working. **❞**

In the first three months in Philadelphia, she roomed with her NOC mates. Then she made a decisive change that typifies what she is all about; she leapt out of her comfort zone in every way.

"I decided to immerse myself with Americans," she said, reasoning that she already saw enough of her NOC mates in class and working on projects. She moved three times in her 18 months there, abandoning the city for the suburbs, where the rent was cheap although the commute was 90 minutes each way. But **"How often in my lifetime could I get to experience living in different places close to a major city?"**

Safety Net for Family

She has never been risk averse although she said she could not always fathom what seemed to her to be the hell-bent for leather approach to starting a business that she kept encountering throughout her time in the US. A Singaporean reaction, perhaps. To Goh, many of those leading start-ups seemed so ready to do everything to get their companies to succeed. She offered the example of Nroute's founder. Because Philadelphia was known to have a start-up-friendly environment, he moved from Alabama (in the south) to launch his business in Philadelphia (in the northeast), some 1,400 km away. He maintained that long-distance relationship for years, was married but had no children.

66 I saw him and others spend their last penny on their start-ups, and many times driving themselves down to the poverty line. 99

"I was thinking to myself, 'Was entrepreneurship like this? So much sacrifice?' I developed my own version of what I think of entrepreneurship in terms of sacrifice."

She rated as "very important" to her NOC experience the ability to see firsthand how entrepreneurs fail — and succeed. The "failure is fine, just move on" culture engendered the "if it doesn't work out, I'd rather die trying than not try at all" spirit that shaped her thinking ahead of her first start-up.

All the same, none of the challenges she saw kept her from plunging headlong into the start-up arena, when she and Nroute's founder started World Indigo to develop roaming services on trains, planes and ferries for mobile phone users. That was in 2004, her fourth and final year. **"Most of Year 4, I was busy with the business."**

World Indigo was up against an immovable obstacle — the Federal Administration Administration's (FAA) ban on using phones on planes. The FAA is an agency of the Department of Transportation which regulates and oversees civil aviation in the US, among other responsibilities.

On reflection, she said, **"We were 10 years too early. It was foolish to go against it. If the law is not on your side, there's nothing more to do."** She left the company and after graduating in May 2005, found a full-time job. Still, that adventure was not a total waste of time. **"It became a case study (at Stanford University) on what could have been done to prevent the failure."**

Yiping, 40, acknowledged without rancour: **"My first two start-ups didn't work out."** In fact, they were just rehearsals for eventual success. The initial setbacks, however, did not make her question her approach or ability. Rather, it all came back to family. Her style of entrepreneurship was to always ensure she had saved enough so that she was financially stable enough to give her parents an allowance.

" I made sure I had one year's worth of savings before I took the plunge. That would provide the safety net for my family because I saw how bad it could be. Entrepreneurship is a tough choice for Asian families, especially Singapore families. My parents had asked me why I wanted to choose this rough road. I wanted to assure my family — and myself — that my own start-up could work. "

There is no doubt that this confluence of crucial factors accelerated her trajectory from hardscrabble working class to modern millennial millionaire. Not, she hastened to add, that she has any intention to stop working. Work is still a consuming passion, as it has been since her childhood.

As the eldest of three children, she worked as cashier, cleaner and kitchen help at her parents' roasted meat hawker stall in Bukit Panjang. She was all of eight years old then.

" I'd have nightmares about giving the wrong change — especially too much change — to customers. During the festive season, I would sell *bak kwa* (roasted meat) on the streets. At the peak, I would also be sent out to spy on the competition, to find out what people were selling and at what prices. "

Later, the family lived in a three-room Housing and Development Board (HDB) flat in Bukit Batok and her father worked two or three jobs to make ends meet. A huge wake-up call came when Goh was 12 and in Primary 6. **"We nearly lost my dad,"** she said. He had a bad fall, slipped into a coma and when he came out of it, his mobility was badly affected. She took on even more responsibility at home while he recovered. The family gave up their stall and her mother went to work for someone else. **"My parents have never complained a single day in their lives,"** she said. They never feared adversity and would work their way through it. Her father recovered and now drives a taxi although the allowance Goh gives her parents obviates the need for them to work.

Among other jobs, she also worked at Singtel's shop, selling mobile phones. **"I enjoyed getting commission on top of a salary. I was among the top three salespersons. And I was the youngest!"**

> ❝ All these experiences were about confidence building, navigating uncertainty and also about the harsh realities of adult life and independent life. What you make is what you enjoy. I financed my own education, through a DBS Bank loan, in my own name. And within two years of my graduation, I paid off the loan. ❞

Goh was fundraising for World Indigo in 2003 when she met the owner of shipping business Pac Leasing (Asia). He had been a banker with Rothschild & Co (UK), **"so I went to him to raise funds."** Instead, her experience as an entrepreneur impressed him so much that he offered her the job of running his shipping business. It was based in the United Kingdom, but he was planning to move the headquarters to Singapore because of its extensive business in China and Southeast Asia.

"Being in the container business and in the Asian time zone, Singapore was strategic for him." She agreed to do it on the condition that she could run World Indigo on the side.

> **❝** I already knew World Indigo didn't have much chance of success unless the FAA reversed its mobile phone ban. I told him that if it closed, I wanted to do the right thing, that is, ensure that my investors could recoup some of what they had put in. **❞**

So, at age 23 she became Managing Director of the new business, IGLU Group, which later became a subsidiary of Rhenus Logistics in Belgium. **"Shipping was new for me, but I pride myself on being able to learn fast."**

She did the job for three years, then gave him a one-year notice of resignation. **"I had saved enough and wanted to launch a business again. I set 2008 as my horizon. He was most unhappy, but we remained good friends."**

Meanwhile, she had already co-founded Human Network Labs with entrepreneur Carlos Garcia in 2007, a tech platform that tracks people and high-value assets using a combination of radio frequency and GPS tech. She had met him in Philadelphia during her NOC stint. **"In 2008, I ran it full time. Carlos was in the US, and I was in Singapore. After I left a couple of years later, he sold it. He made some money. I didn't make anything."**

The Big Deal

Goh's personal story is a classic iteration of the Singapore success paradigm that travels from poverty to possibility and prosperity. She is a near-perfect example of someone who, when presented with a chance, reaches out and seizes it with both hands.

Three was to be her lucky number in terms of start-ups.

The breakthrough came with All Deals Asia, an online aggregator of retail deals. Goh and her brother, Wayne, started it in 2010 when she was 28 and he was 18. The goal: how to find the best promotions without having to trawl through multiple deal sites. By 2012, the site had reached about S$10 million of transactions that were completed at partners' sites. In 2014, All Deals Asia was acquired by Indonesia's Lippo Group, a conglomerate which was estimated to be worth nearly US$1.4 billion in 2020.

66 When we sold All Deals Asia, we were the Number One deal aggregator in Singapore, Malaysia and the Philippines in terms of traffic and subscribers, about 450,000. What set us apart was our first-mover advantage and localised content in each country. The site was also an early adopter of e-services like online customer support. Back in 2010, we provided customers with real-time help when live chat was not as widespread on websites. 99

This time, with the acquisition, she finally reaped a decent harvest on her third foray as a technopreneur. She declined to give a dollar figure but acknowledges that she exited All Deals Asia comfortably as a millionaire.

Part of the deal required Goh to be based in Jakarta for three years to run All Deals Asia and develop the e-commerce business of the new Matahari Mall for Lippo. In 2017, she came home and shortly after, joined Element Inc, a New York-based biometrics artificial intelligence (AI) company on facial recognition. It is one of the most famous AI companies globally, whose co-founder is Yann LeCun, a highly respected AI researcher and entrepreneur based in Canada.

" He hired me to be the President of this company and I was to be based in New York. But because of my Indonesian experience, they kept sending me back to Indonesia. I was pregnant in 2017 and did not think the frequent flying was good. I just wanted to make sure my baby and I were healthy. So, after seven months, I left Element and took a break for two years. "

Moving into the Venture Capital Arena

Over the years in Indonesia, Goh had been dipping her toes into venture capitalism by helping Quest Ventures on the side. She had met its co-founder James Tan at a start-up networking event. They became friends. In 2016, she worked as a freelance venture partner with Quest. Three years later, she joined it full-time. Her role was to pick out early-stage start-ups to invest in and nurture.

Goh sees her venture in Quest as a move that connects the dots, allowing her to use a variety of skills, connections and experiences.

" It is a natural evolution of my journey. It's a place for me to source for new deals. I belong to the start-up world, so it is easy for me to empathise with fellow founders. Quest allows me to give back in the most impactful sense. The brand of venture capitalism that I bring to industry is financial thinking coupled with an operations mindset that we're learning together with the founders. That brand and approach is more bottom-up than top-down. "

She cautioned that entrepreneurship takes a toll on the mind as the idea will evolve or pivot to a point where the founder does not recognise it anymore. She also strongly believed that it is important not to overthink things. **"If you are not my oyster, I'll go to the next oyster."**

NOC now has a strong alumni exceeding 3,600 people and she is the only ex-NOC intern on NUS' Alumni Advisory Board.

❝ I'm a firm believer of being grateful to the provider, where you come from. Thus, I am interested in giving back, to hopefully shape a more connected alumni. I used to think that every NOC alumni has to be an entrepreneur. But in the last few years, the narrative has been changing, there's strength in diversity. I now think that not everyone should become or would become an entrepreneur. We all went through entrepreneurship training, and you can bring this wherever you go. ❞

This evolving narrative shows a maturing in the growth of NOC, she said, as with her personal life. She is married to Carlos Bañón, an architect and associate professor at the Singapore University of Technology and Design. They have one child, and another is on the way. **"My antidote to a bad day is my husband,"** she said with a grin.

As she enters her 40s, Goh remains very much the poster girl for technopreneurship in Singapore. When it was pointed out to her, she responded with a laugh and declared, **"It's time for someone else to take over."**

CHAPTER 9

THE INFLUENCERS III:
The Aljunied Brothers and Mohan Belani

The Aljunied brothers (from left), Muhammad, Ahmed and Ali, have founded among themselves seven tech start-ups in Singapore and Indonesia.

A Family of Entrepreneurs

Aljunied is a name that occupies an illustrious place in the chronicles of Singapore's early history.

Syed Omar Ali Aljunied,[46] a wealthy spice merchant from Sumatra, was Singapore's first Arab trader to settle here soon after the arrival of colonial founder Sir Stamford Raffles in 1819. He went on to own large tracts of land including a huge swathe in present-day Aljunied. He was a philanthropist who donated money as well as land to build madrasahs and religious buildings such as St Andrew's Cathedral and Singapore's oldest mosque, Masjid Omar Kampong Melaka.

His legacy may have contributed to the entrepreneurial spirit in at least three of his younger descendants: Ahmed, 40; Ali, 34 and Muhammad, 29. Among them, they have developed seven tech-related services and products. The innovations include Indonesian property FinTech start-up PinHome, an e-commerce platform that facilitates real estate transactions, and Singapore-based Tagronauts, a software that can print on the spot the required number of copies of a picture taken at an event.

The trio, however, credit their father Abdullah, an electrical engineer, for being the biggest influencer in fostering their entrepreneurial spirit. The 69-year-old is a serial entrepreneur. While running a shipyard business in Malaysia in the early 1980s, he taught himself computer programming from a book. By the late 1980s, he began developing novel solutions for Singapore's events sector, like a fuss-free barcode registration system for participants.

His innovations inculcated in Muhammad a deep desire to solve everyday problems with out-of-the-box solutions.

❝ Dad started getting me involved in his work when I was five. Among other duties, he'd task me to mash keyboards, that is, randomly and erratically press the buttons until errors appeared in his programs. I loved watching him come up with solutions. ❞

LESSONS FROM SILICON VALLEY

The seeds Abdullah planted in his boys blossomed under the NOC programme, which principally taught them how to transform an idea into a sustainable start-up. In the process, they also developed such characteristics as precision, tenacity and risk-taking.

"What my Dad taught us primarily was how to take a product to market," said Ahmed. **"That last mile, of providing a product/service to customers is challenging, and seeing him do it again and again, also in markets completely foreign to him, was inspiring."** It played a leading role in affirming their decisions to be entrepreneurs.

All three interned in Silicon Valley, with oldest brother Ahmed heading to the global centre of technological innovations in 2005, at age 23, to intern at chipmaker Excelics Semiconductor.

"I shared a house with other NOC interns and being away from home, I learnt to be really independent." Also priceless to him was the exposure at close quarters to the challenges the company faced and what it did to survive and thrive. **"The vision and the drive of the founders were awe-inspiring."**

In Silicon Valley, interns had "tremendous access" to business leaders and tech firm founders who readily shared their expertise. **"They'd give us time, a practice that should be transplanted to Singapore,"** he said.

After getting his computer engineering degree, Ahmed worked at enterprise marketing start-up L2 Solutions in the United States. After almost six years, he quit to pursue a Masters in Computer Science at Stanford University. Along the way, he co-founded two start-ups in Indonesia before being hired as the Chief Technical Officer of Jualo.com, an Indonesia-based e-classifieds marketplace for second-hand goods.

In 2017, he joined Indonesia's premier ride-hailing start-up Gojek. As its Vice President of Engineering and Product, he was empowered to operate like a start-up, with the freedom to pursue business opportunities and raise funds for products. He and a team at Gojek's head office established the company's suite of home services, a move that helped uplift a lot of the country's informal service workers. He was the co-leader of two product groups: Lifestyle, which included GoMassage GoClean, GoGlam and GoFix, services that respectively represent massage, home cleaning, salon care and home appliance repair, respectively. The other was Commerce, which included GoMart for grocery delivery and GoShop, a shopping concierge service.

The experience of working in a fast-growing unicorn proved invaluable, he said. The expertise and mindset cultivated from operating as if in a start-up triggered a fervent desire in him to strike out on his own. In 2019, he left Gojek and co-founded Pinhome, Indonesia's largest property e-commerce platform.

HOW AHMED SWAYED YOUNGER BROTHER ALI

Unlike many entrepreneurs, Ahmed had no youthful dreams of being one. He had mapped out a conservative career track for himself, wherein he would get a Singapore-based job at an established tech organisation like Microsoft and climb the ranks.

> 66 But the NOC programme pushed me out of my comfort zone. It showed me that the world is my playground, and that there are no limits and no boundaries. It also instilled a drive and motivation in me to problem-solve. 99

His change of heart and vocal enthusiasm for NOC convinced his younger brother Ali to embark on his own NOC journey. Ali, who was studying computer science at NUS as well, had been contemplating a career in software engineering. But egged on by Ahmed, he attended NOC events to get a sense of the enthusiasm he saw in his brother. He was bowled over.

> 66 The people I met were all trying extremely hard to come up with ideas for start-ups and they didn't care whether it would work. They just kept at it and this drive of technopreneurs to bring their ideas to life — undeterred by setbacks, brickbats and bottom lines — was so compelling that I knew I had to join the community when I graduate. 99

In July 2011, he flew to California for a 12-month internship that was to lay the foundation for his technopreneurship journey. His time at software firm Ensuant, an enterprise software platform, left an indelible impression, especially the friendliness of the founders who invited him to their homes.

❝ On my first day of work, a founder invited me to his home to meet his family and get a taste of life in California, where they have been living for 20 years. We found we liked the same food, like burgers. ❞

Early in the internship, the founders held a meeting with him and offered him shares in the company.

❝ I was surprised. I would be there only for a year, and they were already giving me equity in the company. That demonstrated to me the culture they had over there. It's about appreciation and the value they put on my work. ❞

Today, Ali leads the product and engineering team at Indonesian e-commerce start-up Tinkerlust, where women can buy and sell pre-loved luxury fashion clothes, handbags, shoes and accessories. At the same time, he co-runs Tagronauts with his father. One of his major contributions to this business was to write the live Instagram printing software.

ROCKY START FOR MUHAMMAD, THE YOUNGEST

When it came time for the youngest brother to consider NOC, there was no hesitation as Muhammad had witnessed its impact on the careers and lives of his older brothers.

But his journey was rocky from the start.

After obtaining a Diploma in Information Technology from Temasek Polytechnic in 2012, he wanted to fortify it with a computer science degree from NUS but he did not qualify. Ali took him to meet Associate Professor Ben Leong who taught at the School of Computing and he recommended that Muhammad take computer engineering and then transfer to computer science after the first semester.

But computer engineering proved to be a course that Muhammad liked, so he stayed on.

Likewise, he had failed in his first bid to get into the NOC programme but succeeded on the second attempt.

Muhammad was, in fact, among the last two batches of NOC students to spend a year in the United States before the onset of the Covid-19 pandemic in early 2020. The experience, he added, equipped him with not only the essential marketing skills but also the boldness to network and "sell" himself effectively.

66 Without proper entrepreneurial knowledge, you might find it difficult to overcome roadblocks in your start-up journey. In my father's case, he was often unable to scale beyond a certain number of clients. You can make the best product in the world but if you don't market it, it will all be for naught. NOC showed me how to go to market and grow an idea. The experience also allowed me to immerse myself in an open and communicative culture that is different from Singapore's. It helped build my confidence, which I now apply to any business situation anywhere in the world. 99

After his NOC stint in 2019, Muhammad worked at home in his family's five-room public housing flat in Pasir Ris and developed a customised software that he sold to non-profit organisation LBKM in May 2020. Soon after, it was used at its first pandemic-induced virtual annual general meeting where members were able to vote in secret.

66 Most of the users were elderly folks, above 50 years old. They did not have to deal with passwords; they just registered by keying in their mobile phone number and email. They will receive a digital token that allows them to vote in secret. 99

Muhammad and Ali have since launched shawp.app, an app for home-based businesses to streamline their order and payment processes during the pandemic. If successful, Muhammad envisions it being rolled out in neighbouring countries like Indonesia.

"There is money in innovating," he said. And like the other technopreneurs in his family, this NOC alumni eschews being a 9am to 5pm salaried man. **"I want to be challenged. I don't want to be too comfortable so early in life."**

Mohan Belani, from Geeky Wallflower to Entrepreneur

Growing up, Mohan Belani deliberately avoided large family gatherings and wedding parties. **"With a drink in hand, I would cower in a corner the entire evening and hope no one would notice me, let alone talk to me. I struggled talking to girls. I had no social skills."**

Today, the 39-year-old Singaporean heads one of Asia's largest tech media and networking platforms that serves more than 40,000 start-ups.

The platform, however, had a humble origin. It was a Singapore start-up blog named e27[47] but Belani, teaming up with Thaddeus Koh, rebuilt it into a portal focused on the regional tech ecosystem. To do it so, they raised S$2.5 million from venture capitalists and angel investors.

Belani credits his transformation from geeky wallflower to a go-getting head honcho to his NOC stint in Silicon Valley. He was aged 23 in 2006 and the allure of working among tech giants such as Apple,

Mohan Belani is co-founder and CEO of e27. He is an angel investor and a sought after speaker for his insights on the start-up landscape in the region.

Google and Facebook, and attending courses at Stanford University was irresistible.

He, however, did not reckon with the hard-driving, aggressive networking culture of the world's innovation hub.

❝ But I was lucky. I was paired with a senior in the NOC programme who would threaten, whenever we attended events, not to give me a car ride home unless I collected 10 business cards or talked to at least three people. ❞

His buddy upped the stakes regularly and eventually, Belani was slick enough to work a room of 100 people.

He then set his sights on attending one of the biggest e-commerce shows in New York: Shop.org Annual Summit.[48] But his employer Kriyari Inc., which offered publishers a quick and easy way to embed online stores on their websites, was a fledgling start-up. Its coffers had enough money to buy just one US$3,000 basic pass for the boss to attend the four-day event.

Undeterred, Belani contacted the trade show organiser and pleaded to be a volunteer. **"I also threw in what is viewed as a very prestigious accolade — that I had been given a scholarship to intern in Silicon Valley."** Persuaded, the organiser met him at the registration counter, handed him a USD$5,000 gold pass and said, **"Take this pass and have a great time."**

His first stop was the show's high-level banking event attended by the Who's Who of the industry. During the sessions, he collected 50 business cards and most of them later became clients of Kiyari. **"The event was the golden ticket, a winning move for me because the boss took me along on demo-calls and together, we closed a good number of sales derived from the trade show alone."**

CHAMPIONING THE UNDERDOG

The NOC experiences brought home to Belani the importance of visibility, personal branding as well as deep and meaningful networking.

They paved the way for the founding of e27, a comprehensive tech business development and networking platform for entrepreneurs. Once located in a skyscraper on the fringe of Singapore's Central Business District, the company now operates remotely, with everyone working from home.

Its name is inspired by American venture capitalist Paul Graham.

> ❝ He said youths aged 27 and below are the people to watch and invest in. For instance, the founders of Dropbox and Facebook were young with fresh ideas. They built technology to tackle and disrupt existing industries sans the baggage. ❞

The original e27 — the 'e' stands for entrepreneur — was established by a group of NOC alumni in 2007 for would-be start-ups and entrepreneurs to come together as a community. Five years later, in 2012, Belani and Koh, who is also an NOC alumni turned it into what it is today: a digital marketplace that connects tech start-ups with each other, pairs them with investors and offers job matching services. It also hosts events in Asia.

Since its inception, e27 has grown from a two-worker outfit to an enterprise with about 25 employees. **"Our mission is to empower entrepreneurs with the tools to build and grow their companies, as well as raise Southeast Asia's tech ecosystem to a global level."**

His Silicon Valley stint also opened his eyes to the struggles of a start-up, he said. For instance, Kriyari's office in Palo Alto was a 400 sq ft storage room, which is about the size of a two-room public housing flat. The space was just enough for three people and a small pantry, and it was sited next to a carpark in the basement of a building owned by one of Kriyari's venture capitalists.

With Asia rising, Belani believes Southeast Asia holds tremendous potential and promise. **"Silicon Valley is no longer the sole hub for grooming tech start-ups,"** he said.

66 Southeast Asia is complex from a cultural and market standpoint. To understand the talent and the environment, we will need to spend more time in the region. Going away to Silicon Valley for a year may no longer be as impactful if you're hoping to eventually build a company in Southeast Asia. 99

CHAPTER 10

The Women Entrepreneurs

Audrey Tan co-founded PlayMoolah to teach the importance of financial literacy to children.

Girls tinkering with computers and coding may still be a rare sight in this new century but the gender gap has been steadily narrowing in the NOC programme since its launch in 2002.

Women initially made up about one-third of total participants between 2002 and 2009. But in recent years, the proportion has jumped to 40 per cent between 2015 and 2019 and at the last count earlier this year, women in total comprise 39 per cent of the more than 3,600 alumni. Today, many of them are on top of tech in various sectors of the economy. They either lead businesses as entrepreneurs or head teams in companies as intrapreneurs to create and implement innovative products and services.

Audrey Tan, Charmain Tan, Gwendolyn Regina Tan and Aileen Sim are among them. Their inventions include hand gloves that allow people to type a text message in the cold, and a financial literacy platform that aims to eradicate poverty.

All credit goes to NOC, they said. It not only gave them the skills and tools, but also access to networks, mentors, alumni and thought leaders that were critical in nurturing their ventures during the infancy years. While being a woman may occasionally be an obstacle in an industry accustomed to seeing men as tech titans, it can be overcome with relative ease. **"Just be assertive, they said."** They also advise women to demonstrate a healthy risk appetite, stamina for long working hours and an obsession with creating value for customers.

The overseas stint instilled in them confidence and courage. Audrey Tan, co-founder of PlayMoolah, a social enterprise that develops financial learning tools for young people, said:

> **"** Seeing at close range the commitment of Silicon Valley founders in the way they lead diverse teams, tough it out amid resource shortages and never give up even when they are down to their last dollar gave us NOC students a vivid picture of what it takes to succeed. **"**

But being a young, successful woman entrepreneur comes with some personal sacrifice. Work-life balance is elusive, as is romance, quipped Charmain Tan, the 32-year-old founder of QuickDesk, a software for small and medium-sized enterprises (SMEs) and sales professionals to boost their business. Women who are successful in leading start-ups tend to be highly focused and driven, and the pool of like-minded partners is small, she said, musing that sales is like dating. **"After you get your leads on board, you've got to nurture them, talk to them. Then you convert them. Unfortunately, if you're a woman, taking the initiative to convert a man is a bit tricky."**

The five women, however, are not waiting for Cupid. Since graduating around 10 years ago, they have gone on to build their reputations as leaders in innovation. Here are their individual stories.

Audrey Tan, Teaching the Young about Money

The importance of financial literacy came crashing headlong into the lives of Audrey Tan and her roommate Lee Min Xuan while they were rooming in Silicon Valley. The 2008–2009 NOC alumni watched in horror as the global financial crisis battered and bruised friends and families. But more importantly, it brought into sharp focus their frequent conversations on what they can do to alleviate poverty across Southeast Asia. Teaching the young financial literacy became an immediate goal.

They started "Project Moolah" (moolah is an informal word for money) in their small, rented room in the San Francisco suburbs, using games to teach children and their parents how to manage money wisely. They tested the idea with the daughter of an early paying customer and kids of friends and families. That online product evolved into Playmoolah in Singapore and in 2013, the duo launched Whymoolah, a software their start-up co-developed with DBS Bank for its young adult customers to make informed decisions on milestones such as buying a home, getting married, and becoming parents as well as managing their daily expenses.

In building Playmoolah, Tan was inspired by the Silicon Valley technopreneurs and innovators she met while being a product marketing intern at Qik, a company whose stream-live-video-from-your-phone technology was acquired by Skype in 2011 for US$150 million.

She was especially awed by the Qik leaders' focus on problem-solving and lack of airs and graces, often reminding the staff: **"Don't call me Boss."** Their hard-nosed approach in executing their vision is staggering, Tan added. **"What the founders taught me is that if we believed in what we were doing, we should do it. They made a lasting impression on me."**

She was also struck by how the company responded to challenges. It laid off many of its 50 to 60 employees on its United States and Russian teams in the wake of the 2007–2008 global financial crisis. Only interns stayed.

❝ As a result, we did a lot of things and received about US$1,800 a month in salary, which paid for rent and a car. I was doing a lot of user experience, ensuring that customers received the correct support and were happy with Qik's solutions. I was involved with design and testing of early products with customers to get their feedback on what to incorporate in the final product, marketing, and sussing out potential partnerships for Qik. I had to bring in the early revenues. ❞

But the daily pace of learning from Qik while managing the growing traction of Project Moolah was punishing. They were, however, spurred by the encouraging words of their professor at Stanford University: **"Prof Tom Kosnik opened doors and was readily available to give us advice. His support in the early days inspired us."** In fact, he believed so strongly in their Playmoolah plan that he told the duo to **"go do it".**

The women, in turn, took the bold step and went on six months' leave of absence from NUS to focus on getting their idea off the ground. To stay on in the United States, they extended their H1B1 visas to further develop Playmoolah and look for paying customers and potential investors. Their parents as well as Qik's Chief Executive were among Paymoolah's initial investors who contributed to the "small amount" of funds that helped launch the venture.

When their extended visas expired, they returned to Singapore in 2010, hired two interns and grew their business, working with a network of partners that included banks, digital partners and government agencies like the National Youth Council. The early days, however, were a struggle as consumers could not be persuaded to pay for subscriptions. Despite offering discounts, lowering subscription fees and sending countless emails offering free trials, very few even showed interest, said Tan.

"Ultimately, we found that bank customers would support subscription services."

“ OCBC Bank rolled out online games for children to learn about managing their finances and for parents to teach their kids that they can earn money if they were to complete the chores given to them.

We are now working with other banks to customise the games. Business is growing steadily and we have grown in the last five years from a four-person to a 10-person business.

The company has embarked on on a global strategy to inspire, equip and cultivate good practices of financial-emotional resilience and wellbeing for young people, families and educators. ”

Charmain Tan, Helping SMEs and Sales Professionals Manage Customer Relations

Unlike many NOC alumni who opted for Silicon Valley, Charmain Tan cut her entrepreneurial teeth in Stockholm because she did not have a background in software development.

The Swedish capital is famous for its focus on hardware and among such businesses is a medical technology company called Episurf. It customises 3D-printed implants to replace cartilage defects so that people can avoid total knee replacement. But in August 2010, when the 20-year-old walked through its doors, the company was just two years old. **"I was the fourth person there,"** she recalled. Its Chief Executive Officer (CEO) Nina Blake was only 29 years old.

"My first project was marketing the technology for toe injuries." As it is a smaller joint, it was easier to get clinical trials approved for use, she explained. **"So the toe got to market first."** Soon, she became an ardent fan, moved by the impact of the product on those suffering from osteoporosis, a growing problem in many ageing societies. Another outstanding fact, she noted, is that Blake had no medical background. She was trained in industrial systems engineering.

Charmain Tan's first venture did not succeed. Her next start-up faced a fraud charge in 2018 and her tech team all quit. She borrowed money from her parents and soldiered on. Today the company is stable.

By the time Tan returned home in June 2011, her ambition was crystal clear: to produce something of impact and value, while having fun doing so. She had already taken baby steps towards it in Sweden. The idea came while she was standing in Stockholm's frigid cold and trying to use her mobile phone. **"My gloved fingers did not work on the touchscreen of my iPhone despite the conductive tips of the gloves."** She had bought them from Alibaba's e-commerce site Taobao.

It got her thinking of the frustration of people who spend six months of a year in minus 20-degrees weather. After about a year of working on the problem, she came up with an invention: double-layered touchscreen winter gloves woven with conductive fibres. Its inner gloves used ecologically-manufactured nanotech polyester, while the outer mittens were made of recycled polyester. The hybrid was called ISGloves and to launch it, she started the company Fun in Ecological Tech Textiles (FiETT) with three other NOC students: Fitzkhoon Liang based in Stockholm, Tan Yan Liang in Shanghai and Cia Zhi Yun in San Francisco.

After ISGloves was shortlisted for a European Business Challenge, which is a business plan competition, FiETT received a S$50,000 grant from Spring Singapore[49] to get it going. Later in 2011, it raised about S$600,000 from Singapore venture capital firm Red Dot investments.

But with no textile or manufacturing experience, her company was soon trailing far behind its rivals. As the technology of mobile device touchscreens improved and became more responsive, high-tech mittens became irrelevant. ISGloves floundered. But her financial prudence over the years enabled her to pivot the business into another — and subsequently, more successful — venture in 2014. ISGloves was shut down.

In its place came QuickDesk, a software service that provides sales teams at SMEs with the digital tools and solutions to effectively close sales by automating the sales and marketing processes. **"The solution was created in answer to my own desire as well as I wanted to improve sales processes in my own company,"** Tan said.

The invention propelled the business graduate into the 2019 Forbes' 30 Under 30 Asia list. **"That accolade was a huge boost to my confidence and company."** But not before a new crisis wreaked havoc on the company in 2018, putting her through a wringer which she described as "my all-time low".

Her company was hit with a fraud charge. Its six-person tech team also quit en masse leaving her high and dry to handle the technical problems of clients. On top of these imponderables, she had to take care of day-to-day operations. **"I was overwhelmed. I hardly slept and for six months I worked day and night to save my company. My bank account was in the red, with –$29,"** she recalled. With her back to the wall, she turned to her parents. **"It's the first time I'd asked them for a loan for my business. They came through with the S$50,000 I needed to pay my employees their salaries."**

Such major blows are part of many entrepreneurs' journeys, she said. **"All the entrepreneurs I spoke to say they have gone through such lows."** Since then, she has learnt to focus on managing her finances.

> 66 Pre-crisis, I'd invested almost every dollar I made into the business and did not leave anything for myself. The crisis showed me it was really important to segment my finances. Another important lesson: I'm now super rhythmic about cash flow management and preparing for rainy days. 99

While it was an uphill task navigating back to the road to success, Tan would not have it any other way. **"I believe that wanting to be an entrepreneur is inborn. Grit and tenacity are paramount. We must survive the baptism of fire."**

Gwendolyn Regina Tan, from Entrepreneur to Intrapreneur

From young, Gwendolyn Regina Tan enjoyed unusual pursuits.

At age 4, she was in love with the planets and stars. Then she discovered physics, followed by quantum physics, and when she received her first computer in 1996, at age 12, technology became her new passion and programming languages HTML and JavaScript her abiding interest. But this ceaseless curiosity about what makes the physical world around her tick led to an "intellectually lonely" young life, she said. **"Most times people did not know what I was talking about."**

It, however, cultivated in her an independent streak and an enduring zeal to find her own answers and be her own boss. **"I was always interested in being an entrepreneur."** Destined to launch a start-up, she did so even before she completed her NOC stint in Silicon Valley. The stimulus that set in motion her entrepreneurial journey in 2005 was her blogging hobby. Spotting a gap in the market, she started a tech and entrepreneurship blog, SGEntrepreneurs (SGE).

Gwen Tan has always wanted to be her own boss. In her 17-year working journey, she has stayed in the start-up ecosystem. She has been a co-founder, a partner in a venture capital firm and a leader in other start-up firms. Today, she is investment director, Binance.

❝ Traditional media was covering the big companies. Start-ups and tech developers were very small businesses but they needed the publicity. I felt it's important to highlight the uncelebrated stories about those who were driving innovation in small ways. Also, I like writing, I like tech and I like innovation. **❞**

Like other entrepreneurs, she suffered financial setbacks, received support from unexpected quarters and experienced happy endings.

Her start, however, was relatively smooth, she said. On returning home from Silicon Valley in 2006, she co-founded Thymos Capital, an early-stage technology investment firm in Singapore. She was just 22 years old. Without a mound of money for capital, she and her founding partners tapped into a government micro-funding programme called i.JAM to invest in digital start-ups.

For every company Thymos invested in, it would receive a $10,000 management fee, out of which it would invest S$5,000 in the company. **"The economics was almost too good to be true; the government was trying to seed the next Google and they built up a system to incentivise private players properly."**

After four years and with the company in a stable state, Tan turned her attention to building up SGE, which had been gaining traction. But it was 2010, and the global financial crisis had yet to run its course. SGE, like almost everyone else, was struggling to stay afloat. She was forced to delay paying her workers their salaries. **"I would say to them, 'I'm so sorry, we were supposed to receive payment but we still haven't,'"** she recounted, wishing then that she had a business coach to guide her on what to do. **"It's a horrible feeling, because it's all on me and you start to ask yourself where you've gone wrong."**

Her staff, however, were surprisingly understanding. **"I had such good support from them. They said, 'We know you're trying your best to make things work. We can see it. Don't worry about it.'"**

Finally, in September 2013, she and the other two co-founders sold the website to Singapore-based Tech in Asia, the leading online English-language technology media company in Asia, for an undisclosed sum. She joined the Tech in Asia team as its Business Development Manager for a year before moving to American company Mashable to lead its expansion in Asia.

The job offer from the global, multi-platform media and entertainment company, which is headquartered in New York, came after casual drinks with the man who would be her future boss. He had told her, **"With your entrepreneurial experience, we think you'd be a good fit."**

The whiff of a new adventure proved irresistible. **"I like business development, and the regional and global aspects of the business. It was also a chance to work in a fast-growing company. When I joined in 2015, Mashable had 150 people. When I left in 2017, it had 300 people."**

Indeed, after the Mashable stint, she no longer rules out working for an established company, as long as she can function as an entrepreneur within its framework.

❝ Being an employee driving innovation in an organisation's established framework calls for a different set of skills than in a start-up, where everything has to be built from scratch, with fewer resources and one person carrying out several different functions. In an established company, roles and functions are defined and culture and values established, so a different skillset is needed. What was especially useful for me is to be flexible in my thinking. Fortunately, my NOC experience had prepared me for this, being an entrepreneur and intrapreneur. ❞

However, getting into and staying on the NOC programme was no walk in the park for Tan. She was rejected initially. She applied again in the third year of her liberal arts studies at NUS. She succeeded. Then, almost as soon as she landed in California in July 2005, she had a rental dispute with her landlord. She found new accommodation but the internship job at E-Book Systems, an e-book company, was about a 10-minute drive away. She had to learn to drive.

She had chosen the Singaporean company, whose sales office was in Silicon Valley, because its books, in PDF format, could be opened on mobile devices, including flip phones. In her 12 months there, she learned one invaluable skill: speaking to potential customers.

> **I had to make cold calls to strangers and attend networking events. It was nerve-wracking, very scary. Americans didn't understand my accent or thought my English wasn't good. But being immersed in the culture, talking and networking with Americans taught me a lot. I also learnt from my sales colleagues. All in, it was an interesting learning experience.**

Currently, the 38-year-old is Investment Director at crypto exchange firm Binance. Like many NOC alumni, she has a finger in more than one pie. She is part of an angel syndicate called ghi.vc which invests between S$10,000 and S$250,000 in start-ups and Sandbox, a global community of young leaders. She was also entrepreneur-in-residence until September 2019 at Entrepreneur First, a company that brings together scientists, engineers and technologists to build deep tech companies.

Tan credited NOC for giving her these options to contribute to the Singapore tech ecosystem as well as make some of her best friends. **"As NOC matures, I hope to see its global networks expand."**

Aileen Sim, Tech Start-up Coach

When Aileen Sim entered NUS in 2003, her goal was to get a first class honours in applied mathematics and land a stable job in the public sector. Business had no appeal for her.

> 66 Growing up, money was often an issue in my family as my mother was the only one who works, earning about $2,000 a month. So I had a bad impression of business as it does not assure a steady income. 99

A couple of years later, her plans were upended by her NOC stint in Philadelphia. She no longer wanted to do her honours degree. **"I just wanted to keep working and start a company immediately after graduation."** Which she did in 2006 when she co-founded First Meta. It created an online multi-world currency exchange called First Meta Exchange, which trades both real and virtual currencies.

Having been part of the founding teams, Aileen Sim is using her experiences to coach start-up teams and founders.

People did not take her seriously at the start, she said, until the company gained traction with international media such as TechCrunch, Wired, BBC, and BusinessWeek. Sim sold her stake in FirstMeta in 2011 for a few hundred thousand dollars, went travelling for six months and returned home to join her second start-up, BillPin, in 2012, an early form of PayLah. BillPin was a digital payment platform co-founded by NOC alumni Darius Cheung.

By now, having pioneered two start-ups in Singapore, she felt the pull of the San Francisco Bay Area where Silicon Valley looms large. It was love at first sight, she said with a laugh. **"It was such a melting pot of people and ideologies. Everything was accepted. It's little wonder it became the mecca for technologists and innovators,"** she added. **"Over the years, I've made it my second home. A huge chunk of my friends are from the Bay Area."** She probably saw the irony as she blithely recounted how she dismissed her NOC advisors' recommendation and "stubbornly" insisted on going to Bio Valley in Philadelphia instead of Silicon Valley.

Over the years, she has moved from company to company in her quest to make an impact on people's lives by shaping their environment and using technology to build products they can use. **"Product management is my passion, not managing a business."**

The companies where she had worked included Glow, a data-driven women's health and fertility company in San Francisco, and AirHelp in New York, a start-up that helps travellers claim compensation for delayed, cancelled or overbooked flights. She has also worked at two software companies founded by NOC alumni: PatSnap, the first NOC-supported unicorn, and Saleswhale, an artificial intelligence platform that automates sales emails.

Today, she has funnelled her experiences to coach start-up teams for success, as part of her way to give back for the support she had received. **"The founders' journey is very hard and lonely. You can't confide in employees or co-founders, friends or families,"** she pointed out.

66 The NOC friendships are the only ones we can share and talk frankly. Knowing that you're in the trenches together is very comforting. And hands down, the strongest support came from NOC peers who had started companies around the same time as me.

Even though we were all busy with our own start-ups, there was camaraderie. A sense that we're all trying to do this together and that we've got each other's back. That was so, so important since back then, friends and family didn't always understand why we chose to start companies instead of getting high-paying jobs in banking, consulting or government. 77

That support continues till today, 15 years after her NOC stint, she said.

66 Many of my jobs I got through the NOC network. Today, we're friends who've attended each other's weddings and baby celebrations, who've celebrated our successes together and consoled each another during our failures. 77

CHAPTER 11

WAVING THE FLAG OVERSEAS:
Chean Yujun and Mai Nguyen

Chean Yujun credits the NOC network for helping him find the right contacts to start his insurance tech start-up in 2018. In 2019, he relocated to Thailand to expand the business. He has sold his company to another start-up but continues working as he finds satisfaction from building new business teams.

Beyond Singapore, the NOC programme can be found in more than 15 locations, ranging from Association of Southeast Asian Nations (Asean) countries, India and China to as far as Europe and North America. A survey of its alumni shows that of the alumni based overseas, 15.2 per cent are start-up founders while 17.2 per cent are working in start-ups, according to a 2018 NUS Enterprise survey.[50]

Among them is electrical engineering graduate Sriram Krishnan, 37, who had taken on roles in business development and product management in start-ups in China, Europe and the United States. The companies in which the Malaysian had worked included game developer Cmune in Beijing, music streaming service Spotify in Singapore and dating site Tinder in Silicon Valley.

He is now keeping himself busy as an investor, mentor and advisor to start-ups.

The path he took is not common among the alumni, the survey shows. Most did not plunge immediately into establishing a start-up after graduating. When they eventually did, the majority would found their start-ups in Singapore. Among the entrepreneurs who started their ventures overseas, one in five were likely to have done so in the city where they had done their NOC stint.

The survey also shows a higher chance of alumni becoming entrepreneurs four to six years after they graduate. Chean Yujun, 36, and Mai Nguyen, 35, typify this group. Both were mechanical engineering graduates. Chean founded his insurance company in Singapore eight years after getting his degree in 2008 while Nguyen made her debut in Vietnam about five years after graduating. Each went on a different journey to create their vision of entrepreneurship.

Chean Yujun, Thailand: Helping Drivers Save On Car Insurance

Chean Yujun's ambition to be a tech entrepreneur was sparked in 2006 during his NOC stint. It convinced him that he had the grit and perseverance to start and grow a business, as well as the mindset to never stop scaling up his skills.

But he meandered into three vastly different jobs before becoming a start-up founder. They range from corporate investment banking to business development in a data science start-up. **"By then, I was already 32, going on 33, and I remembered telling myself that if I wanted to strike out on my own, it had to be now."** So in 2016 he co-founded a motor insurance start-up in Singapore that expanded into Thailand in 2018.

Chean praised the NOC programme for giving him new skills and gaining entry into the network of alumni, tech leaders and officials who played a vital role in paving the way for him to achieve his dream.

It began with online marketer eGrabber, which sells software tools for companies to build customer databases. He was its customer service executive who did telephone sales as well. He also revamped its corporate website and conducted product training for customers.

> 66 I remember eGrabber CEO Chandra Bodapati telling me that I was like a lemon — if I had allowed it, he would have squeezed even harder to get more juice. But I was a willing lemon because I wanted to learn. 99

One major skill he acquired was in telephone sales. As a third-year engineering student, he had neither sales nor marketing skills. His sales record was dismal, forcing him to change tactics. Instead of phoning potential customers with a sales pitch, he would start by chatting with them about the weather or sport, to build rapport. **"I learnt to listen more, talk less and make appropriate remarks."** It worked.

His adeptness at sales and customer engagement would subsequently sharpen his entrepreneurial edge, he said.

Chean also stumbled on a new pursuit: Climate change. He came across Energy Crossroads, while attending classes at Stanford University. Inspired by the society's mission to promote sustainable energy, he volunteered at a 2007 conference in Santa Clara,[51] where he heard former American Vice President Al Gore give his speech on global warming. Shortly after, he watched Gore's Oscar-winning documentary, *An Inconvenient Truth*, and was stirred by its message that individuals can play a role in tackling the crisis.

Back home for his final semester, he lost no time in setting up non-profit Energy Carta with five NUS students to educate youth on opportunities in the sustainable development industry and develop young leaders in the field.

Its first project was to organise a conference to connect students with the industry, for which Chean and his team, with the backing of NUS Enterprise, raised about S$200,000. It was a major success, with support from government agencies, such as regulator Energy Market Authority, and national investment strategist Economic Development Board. Commercial sponsors also came forward, including a major airline that flew in the speakers for free. Students from Denmark and the United States were among the international participants.

THE VALUE OF THE NOC NETWORK

Chean's interest in sustainability caught the eye of Singbridge International, a provider of sustainable urban solutions globally. He was hired in early 2009 to help create eco-urban solutions for the company's projects in China.

Before long, he received job offers from two companies and each time, it was an alumni who sought him out. One was at Citi in Singapore and the other at Swiss company Teralytics, a data science start-up that was setting up its Asian operations in Singapore. At Citi Singapore, he was working in corporate banking when Teralytics wooed him to be its head of new markets.

His biggest takeaway from the Swiss start-up was how the founders and senior management worked relentlessly to build the business. It taught him an unforgettable lesson: Founders must have the vision and the gumption to try new things as well as the insight to build capable and cohesive teams.

Ready to put it into practice, he went into insurance. His research had shown an industry that was slow to adopt data applications. Premiums were still based on mortality tables. It was ripe for disruption and Chean felt primed to do it as he was turning 33.

Again, another alumni emerged from the NOC network to give him a hand. Christopher Neo, an insurance underwriter who did his internship in Shanghai between 2006 and 2007, sat next to him at their friend's wedding dinner. They hit it off and for the next three to four months, they met every other weekend for Chean to bone up on insurance and the industry.

" This period was pivotal in accelerating my learning of insurance. Chris provided the context for insurance, how pricing and claims were done and helped me build a business plan. He played a critical role. "

It was timely as well. The word "insurtech", or insurance technology, had just emerged in the start-up lexicon, prompting Chean to register Vouch Insurtech in Singapore in late 2016 as an innovative car insurance social platform. It would incentivise safe drivers with a rebate of up to 12 per cent of their annual car insurance premiums if no claims were made in a 12-month period.

As with his Energy Carta project, NUS Enterprise came to his aid, with a S$10,000 Practicum Award to validate the business idea. He roped in two co-founders: software engineer Prateek Jogani in Bangalore who was introduced to him by angel investors, and Thanasak Hoontrakul, a Thai who was an NOC alumni and student leader in Energy Carta.

The trio spent over a year developing the algorithms and analytical technology for the cashback service, working out of NUS Enterprise incubator The Garage in Kent Ridge. By February 2018, Vouch was launched as Singapore's first car insurance with the "No Claim Rebate" feature. The policy was sold by three partner insurers: NTUC Income, Sompo Insurance Singapore and Tokio Marine Insurance.

Building the business, however, was a daunting task. Besides the prohibitive cost of buying Facebook and Google advertisements, Vouch also faced a formidable rival, FWD, a digital insurance start-up. Its owner was Hong Kong tycoon Richard Li, younger son of billionaire Li Ka-shing, and he had a huge war chest to undercut the market.

Convinced that Vouch could turn the corner with a bigger market, Chean set his sights on Thailand, which has almost 40 million cars against one million in Singapore. Its motor insurance business amounts to about US$4.5 billion annually against Singapore's US$0.8 billion. The average number of yearly Thai claims, however, is 65 for every 100 vehicles versus Singapore's 15. But many claims were small and Chean believed the "No Claim Rebate" model could discourage these claimants.

In mid-2018, Vouch entered Thailand, with Hoontrakul playing a lead role in developing the business. With NUS Enterprise's help, Chean and his three employees set up an office on the top floor of Chulalongkorn University, a 19-storey building in Bangkok's central business district. The space was rent-free, because of an agreement between the University and NUS Enterprise to support each other's start-ups when they expand into the other's country.

The association with the prestigious university also burnished the reputation and legitimacy of Chean's start-up.

In the new environment, Chean was inspired to adopt a new business strategy. Instead of selling to individual car owners, he worked closely with Thai insurance companies and the financial regulator to develop a digital platform for insurers and their agents to sell policies effectively and conveniently to motorists. He renamed the company Fairdee Insurtech in 2018 and closed down the Singapore company soon after.

Fairdee became the first FinTech to operate in a regulatory sandbox set up by the Thai authorities, which enabled it to do live experiments in a controlled environment. Within a few months, its products were approved for launch and insurance agents began to use Fairdee's portal to get the best quotes on car premiums. They would also register the sale on the portal. Separately, Fairdee offered motorists who do not file claims a maximum cashback of 30 per cent of their annual premiums.

Business was brisk. The pandemic gave it a further impetus. In 2020 and 2021, the insurers introduced Covid-19 policies that gave pay-outs to motorists and customers infected by the virus. **"There was a lot of paranoia and insurers made a lot of money. As an insurance broker, our revenue went up, too."**

By August 2020, Fairdee's year-on-year revenue had tripled. But just as he was preparing to raise US$3 million to expand the business, Hoontrakul quit to pursue a Masters in Business Administration abroad. Other companies began to poach his staff as well and soon, he felt burnt out from being in charge of operations and strategy.

His staff, however, coaxed him to reduce his workload and stay. He did. And towards the end of 2020, he accepted an offer from Indonesian insurtech start-up Qoala to buy Fairdee for a confidential amount.

Chean still runs the Thai operations, on top of holding a new portfolio at Qoala: Group Chief Strategy Officer.

Reflecting on his ups and downs, Chean said he would probably not have become an entrepreneur had he not seen an NOC poster at a campus bus stop while returning to his student dormitory in Raffles Hall. **"It had three phrases: Silicon Valley, NUS Overseas College, California. I immediately thought of the American TV series *Baywatch*, with its 'eye candy' lifeguards. I decided to check it out."**

On a more serious tone, he added:

> ❝ The NOC experience gave me the courage to speak up, do something new, embrace change and take on the unknown. You can't plan for these skills; you have to go and do it. Equally important is the NOC and NUS network. Whether you want to call it fate, luck or serendipity, the contacts came through whenever I needed help or was at a crossroad. ❞

Mai Nguyen, Getting Vietnamese Youths to Re-Discover their Cultural Heritage

When Vietnamese Mai Nguyen[52] arrived at NUS in 2006, the first-year mechanical engineering major in mechatronics was set on a career in engineering — but as an academic. It was a goal shaped by her father, who had relocated his wife and three daughters to Adelaide, Australia, to complete his doctorate in linguistics and be an academic.

But the dream evaporated soon after she joined the NUS Entrepreneurship Society and heard about NOC. The women members she met aspired to run their own business, spurred by role models like Elim Chew, who was then a poster girl for entrepreneurship among the young in Singapore. Chew had founded streetwear chain 77th Street in 1988 at age 22.

Amid the buzz, Nguyen met NOC alumni and Playmoolah's co-founder Lee Min Xuan, who recommended her for a 2008 study trip to Silicon Valley organised by the society. Hence, at age 20, she found herself in San Francisco, learning about the start-up culture, visiting tech behemoths such as Google, Apple and Oracle, and marvelling at their brightly-coloured offices and well-stocked pantries.

But it was a visit to the Delancey Street Foundation that opened her world to new possibilities. The self-help organisation for the down and out, such as the homeless, substance abusers and ex-convicts, introduced her to the vitality of social entrepreneurship. **"I felt it was meaningful to combine entrepreneurship with social impact and work on something that would make a difference in people's lives."**

In her final year, she applied for a NOC internship. Silicon Valley, however, was not her top choice. She preferred learning more about low-cost innovation, enticed by the prospect of innovating for a developing country with a big population. **"India was then known for bottom-up innovation. And for the NOC batch in the subcontinent, India was uncharted, and exciting because of that."**

Her stint landed her in India's high-tech hub Bangalore where newcomer Robots Alive was making low-cost robotic arms that could be manipulated. **"The founders were enthused by the idea of someone coming from Singapore to join them,"** she said, recalling the start-up had only five people, all men.

Its mission was to develop a low-cost robotic arm for local businesses and educational institutions. **"I was a technical intern during my three-month attachment and my job was to look into algorithms of how to program a robotic arm to achieve a certain position."**

While the work and living environment was scruffy and took some getting used to, the eco-friendly ways of the warm and welcoming rural folk were a pleasant surprise.

She was among nine NOC interns in Bangalore at that time and would travel by bus or rickshaw to her spartan office furnished with old and used furniture. Once, a woman in an overly crowded bus invited Mai to sit on her lap. She declined.

On another occasion, **"as we went past a wedding celebration, the people invited us to join them. I saw that all their plates were made of woven leaves."** It was part of their philosophy of *jugaad*, a colloquial Hindi word for frugal innovation, which adopts a flexible approach to problem solving by using limited resources in innovative ways. It became the guiding light in her entrepreneurial journey, she said, as being adaptable and able to work with a diverse group of people is crucial to overcome the frequent shortages of resources that start-ups face.

Back in Singapore in 2011, she took a job as a commissioning robotics engineer at global robotics company ABB where potential customers would give her specifications of the products they needed.

After four years, she quit and returned home to Vietnam and made her first foray into the world of social enterprise. In May 2015, she became a FabMaster at Fablab Saigon, a place where students, engineers and hardware entrepreneurs can congregate and produce environmentally-friendly widgets or products that also help disadvantaged communities.

Next, she joined FabAcademy[53] Taipei as a long-distance student to get better at digital fabrication and learn how to translate ideas to products.

Soon, Mai was itching to do her own thing and started a social enterprise to revive and preserve Vietnamese cultural heritage. Based in Ho Chi Minh City, it offers youths hands-on experience in making traditional products. She named it INGO — an acronym for a Vietnamese phrase that means printing with wood — and began with the ancient folk art of woodblock painting, whose birthplace is Dong Ho village in Hanoi.

With donor funds, she began fabricating educational do-it-yourself kits for children aged six to 10 to create traditional prints in a classroom with their teachers, or at home with their parents.

The pandemic may have delayed some expansion plans, but the ideas for innovation keep on coming, she said, attributing the mindset to her NOC stint.

66 It develops one's frame of mind to see the whole world as your playground, and that you can be anywhere and work with anyone. This global outlook is what NOC and NUS in general have given me — and I'm thankful for it. 99

THE NEXT 20 YEARS

CHAPTER 12

Covid-19 Upheavals

Pratyay Jaidev (right) was recalled to Singapore together with other NOC students from Munich.

When the Pandemic Struck

The air in Shanghai was thick with the festive joy of Chinese New Year. The festival was about a week away and Gary Teo was packing his thick woollies to spend the holidays in Harbin, China's north-eastern city famed for its Ice and Snow Sculpture Festival. Together with two fellow National University of Singapore (NUS) Overseas Colleges (NOC) interns, they were scheduled to fly to the winter wonderland on the eve of Chinese New Year.

But it was not to be. Instead, the trio was plunged into a frantic search for a flight home to Singapore.

"We didn't know whether we could fly tomorrow, the day after tomorrow or weeks later," said Teo, recalling the struggle to get a plane ticket in January 2020 amid the deteriorating Covid-19 situation in China.

66 NOC in Singapore had told us, in no uncertain terms, to catch the first available flight home. But airlines had begun to reduce the number of daily international flights. And to make matters worse, the flights were invariably full because Singaporeans living in China were also going back to celebrate the festival with family. Some were also not taking chances with the then little-known virus. 99

Finally, on the eve of Chinese New Year, Teo, with a repacked suitcase, boarded a Singapore Airlines flight home. The plane landed in Singapore on 25 January, the first day of the new year festivities.

"Looking back, I'm glad I got out in the nick of time," said the third-year NUS Project and Facilities Management student. By 23 January, China had locked down Wuhan, the provincial capital where the virus had allegedly originated. Four days later, on 27 January, the entire province of Hubei, with more than 57 million people, was under lockdown.

Meanwhile, Singapore had required all arrivals from China who displayed symptoms to be isolated. Teo went to his parents' home in Yishun directly from the airport to serve his two-week Stay-Home Notice at home.

The government also advised Singaporeans against making non-essential trips to Hubei as Singapore announced its first cases of the coronavirus on 23 January. All seven of them were Chinese nationals from Hubei.

A week later, on 1 February, Singapore barred people of all nationalities with recent travel history to mainland China from entering or transiting in Singapore. Measures to combat the virus were progressively tightened in February. Still, the numbers kept climbing up and by the end of the month, Singapore had more than 100 cases.

While Asia was initiating battle-ready measures, the United States (US) and Europe hardly took notice of the virus. Pratyay Jaidev, a third-year computing science student at NUS, had arrived in Munich in February 2020 to intern at data science company Erium and had plans to make weekend visits to London to explore its museums and attend rock concerts.

But within four weeks of his arrival, he received the dreaded call. **"I remember it was Friday, 13 March. My friends and I were discussing going to London for a pop concert when we received an email from NOC informing us to prepare for the recall."**

Three days later, he flew home, arriving on 17 March and was placed on quarantine for two weeks. It was an abrupt end to his internship which came about 11 months earlier than the scheduled February 2022.

Not knowing when they would return to Germany, Jaidev and his friends spent their last weekend in Munich quaffing German beer and eating their fill of German sausages and sauerkraut. They also binged on many packets of instant noodles left behind by a previous resident of the flat.

Operation Recall

It is perhaps no small irony that NOC had to manage the first major disruption to its programme on the fly, a response most founders of start-ups would say is par for the course. Even the 2003 severe acute respiratory syndrome (SARS)[54] outbreak, which had originated in China, was, on reflection, a mild rehearsal. It had remained largely in Asia, lasted about five months, from February to July, and affected only one cohort of NOC students.

The Covid-19 pandemic, on the other hand, began spreading in December 2019, reached almost every corner of the world and has yet to be tamed as of the time of writing.

Professor Chee Yeow Meng, NOC's Director, recalled the tumultuous time as he and the programme's senior managers grappled with the complex task of ensuring the students' safety and well-being. Initially, it meant closely monitoring developments in China, getting updates from the World Health Organization (WHO) and keeping in close contact with the students. The 239 interns in 10 countries would receive regular phone calls and text messages to ensure that they were fine, physically and mentally, even as they were forewarned to be prepared to fly home at short notice.

The call to return home came five days after China confirmed the human-to-human transmission of the virus on 19 January. With immediate effect, Singapore's Ministry of Education (MOE) suspended all student exchange programmes with China.

In the next two months, the disease spread throughout the world. The WHO deemed the disease a pandemic on 11 March. On 13 March, Prof Chee emailed NOC interns saying, **"We now feel it is prudent and urgent to recall all overseas NOC students."**

The risk of the students being stranded, as countries started imposing lockdowns, border closures and travel curbs, was **"just too high"**, he added.

The following day, MOE sent out a directive requiring all Singapore students at overseas institutions of higher learning to return as soon as possible.

By 23 March 2020, all 239 NOC students were back in Singapore. They were part of Singapore's biggest evacuation of its people working and studying abroad, with free flights offered to bring them home.

Managing Upset Students

Some of the NOC interns, however, questioned the wisdom of the move. They felt that it was safe to remain overseas. Others were worried about fulfilling their required academic credits. There was also the financial cost of breaking a rental contract and shipping their belongings home. But the grief felt by all was the loss of the opportunity to grasp what makes entrepreneurs in leading tech cities tick, learn new skills and build a network of new contacts.

Prof Chee, Ho Geer How (NOC's regional director for Asia) and other NOC managers spent weeks addressing their concerns. Prof Chee pledged that their absence in classes abroad would not affect their academic credits. They would also be reimbursed for expenses on airline tickets, rent deposits and mobile phone fees, and their internship would continue, but remotely in Singapore.

The other daunting task was bringing the students home and ensuring they did not break the quarantine rules. **"It was operationally complex because of the uncertainty and fluidity of the situation. Also, the students initially did not understand the seriousness of the situation,"** said Ho. He, too, did not initially see the need for a recall. During the 2003 SARS crisis, he had been working as an engineering manager in China and had seen the outbreak being overcome in six months.

As the Covid-19 situation worsened, the NOC set up a cloud command centre headed by Prof Chee, with support from a team comprising Ho and colleagues that included Gay Peng Kee, Sherine Koh and Mak Hui Min.

Ho focused on getting the interns home.

The first step was to discuss the travel arrangements with them. It would appear easy enough, except that in China, students were on the road during the Chinese New Year holidays and had no access to the Internet, thus rendering them uncontactable.

The problem, which was resolved in a few days, was among a string of challenges. One of them was border chaos as some places revised their travel restrictions more than once a day, while others closed their borders indefinitely. Another was airlines continually changing their flight schedules, if not stopping flights altogether to certain destinations.

Yet another was quarantine. Students could serve their Stay-Home Notice at their own home or in NUS hostels in College Green or Prince George's Park. Some stayed in hotels when the hostels were full. Prof Chee had specially catered for their three daily meals while Ho met them on arrival with a welfare pack containing necessities such as thermometers, electrical adapters and plugs for charging electronic devices.

To ease mental strain, a 24-hour hotline was set up for students to air any problem or issue that irked them. At least once a day, each student would receive a call from the NOC team to ask how they were faring.

"Initially, they were cheerful and would chit chat with us," said Prof Chee. **"By the fourth day, they were less chatty. We would tell them jokes and talk about all kinds of topics."**

One student sneaked out of his room and was caught on the hotel's CCTV climbing down the fire escape. He told Prof Chee that he had wanted to go for a smoke. Another walked to a nearby hawker centre to eat. Some walked to the convenience store outside the hotel or visited each other in their rooms. A few were locked out of their rooms — without masks — because they had forgotten their key cards, while a handful were caught strolling maskless in the hotel foyer. **"The students just did not understand the seriousness and enormity of the pandemic,"** said Ho.

Prof Chee added:

>   We had to report to NUS management those who had just walked out of their hostel or hotel rooms. They were disciplinary cases because they could spread the virus. Altogether, seven students were suspended for one to two semesters.

Out of the 239 students recalled, six were infected by the virus.

Burden of Bringing Home the Belongings

With many cities in complete or semi-lockdown, hired contractors were hampered in packing and collecting the students' belongings. Tsinghua University in Beijing, for example, was locked down, with all outsiders barred from entering the hostel rooms of the NOC students. After much coaxing, the university allowed the hostel friends of the students to pack the belongings and take the boxes to a specified exit, where the contractor collected them for shipment to Singapore.

The collection was less complicated when it involved private apartments. NUS collected the keys from the students who had returned home and sent the keys by courier to the logistics contractors in China. When the contractors were in the apartments, they would receive instructions via video calls from the students on what to pack. This was largely the case in the US and Europe, too.

Navigating the lockdowns, border closures and reduced international flights resulted in the bags and boxes arriving in Singapore in April 2020, almost two months after the students had returned home.

It would be another couple of months before they could collect them as Singapore's Circuit Breaker rules disallowed outdoor movements except for essential services. Ho had the 151 suitcases and boxes stored at a warehouse in Changi Airport.

When the Circuit Breaker was lifted in June 2020, the items were taken to The HANGAR, a start-up office on NOC's premises on the NUS campus.

Yet another set of ground rules was imposed to prevent intermingling among students during collection. Each was given a specified time to collect their bags, which were laid out in the car park outside The HANGAR. They had to turn up in motor vehicles and cruise around the car park to locate their belongings. They were not allowed to get out of their vehicles. When they had identified their bags, Ho would carry them to the students.

The cost of packing, shipping and storing the belongings amounted to almost S$40,000. NUS paid the bill.

Interning on Home Ground

Interns who returned from China in January were initially offered stints in neighbouring countries like Vietnam or a two-week study tour of Israel and Germany to visit the start-ups there.

Teo, who was interning as an account executive at advertising firm Contact Media in Shanghai, opted for an internship in Ho Chi Minh City. On 15 March 2020, he flew to Vietnam. But the pandemic again derailed his overseas stint. The day after he departed, MOE informed all Singapore students on overseas placements, including those on internships and exchange programmes, to return home. Teo was back in Singapore the following day. **"I had been away a mere 48 hours."**

The study tour of start-ups in Israel and Germany also did not materialise.

About 120 students completed their internship by working remotely with the overseas start-up companies they had interned with, and nine either withdrew or were terminated from the programme. The remaining 113 continued their internships at local companies. **"They were very supportive,"** said Xander Khoo, NOC's programme manager for Singapore. **"Many had previously taken in NOC interns and some were founded by NOC alumni."** The companies included 2359 Media, 99.co, Circles.Life, Endofotonics, Haulio, SWAT Mobility and Quest VC. Teo completed his internship with local educational technology start-up KooBits.

Lesson on Racism

The chief lesson from the pandemic, said Prof Chee, was that the students needed to be better prepared for their overseas internships. One area is how to handle racism. Those who are ethnically Chinese can run into racism in the US and Europe because of reports and some foreign political leaders repeatedly pointing to China as the source of the virus. **"We had to teach the students how to manage such situations,"** he added.

In 2021, as the pandemic persisted, NOC ran the internship programme remotely, replicating as much of the overseas experience as possible for the students. They had access to the same group of mentors and coaches in each NOC location and engaged with the entrepreneurs and venture capitalists over Zoom. They were also able to take available courses, but virtually, at the NOC partner universities.

It became evident from the pandemic that whatever the crisis, the NOC programme will proceed unabated, said Prof Chee. It had proven to be an influential force behind many start-ups in Singapore, including two companies that are valued at more than US$1 billion: Carousell and PatSnap.

NUS promptly switched back to overseas attachments when it became possible for students to travel again.

In October 2021, 19 months after the interns were recalled home, the NOC programme resumed its overseas attachments. Fifty-five fully vaccinated students left for Silicon Valley, New York, Stockholm, Munich and Toronto.

These NOC students were among many who received virtual pre-departure briefings on Zoom.

The sense of wonder while abroad changes the students and they return bubbling with ideas and the derring-do, know-how and confidence to turn new ideas into products and services, said Prof Chee.

❝ There are certain things that come with onsite location — the adventure and discovery of living and working overseas where every step is an adventure. ❞

NUS, meanwhile, has set up a monitoring system to track border policies, the pandemic situation, vaccination regime and safe management measures in the cities where the students are interning. Their health and well-being are also monitored regularly, and they would be brought home immediately should the situation warrants it, Prof Chee added.

In January 2022, another group of about 50 students left for the US, Germany, Sweden and Canada.

With the re-opening of borders, the NOC programme is on track to resume full operations.

m 1-2 Jarren Koh
3-4 Daniel Foong Wee Keong
3-4 Patcha Chow
3-3 Chia Chu You
2-2 Ong Jing Qing, Karen
Dionne Poon Yuxian
1-2 Bryan Wong Hong Liang
1-5 - Shiyun Huang
Mai Xueqiao
2-4 Teh Ru En
m 2-4 -Muhammad Niaaz Wahab
3-3 Justin Loh
1-1 - Anthony Xavier Poh Tianci
2-4 irene wong
3-4 Ho Han Fan
m 4-2 Lim An Qi
2-5 Jasmine Chen Yu Qing
Jared Cheang
smridhi patwari
4-4 Tan Yi Wei
Team 4-4 Jolene...
3-3 - Hui Ling Sh
m 2-3 Yong Ming Yang
1-2 M Farhana
2-3 Ang Yang Cheng
Team 4-4 Jolene Lam
3-3 - Hui Ling Shi

CHAPTER 13

SUCCESS OF NOC Emboldens NUS

NOC resumed its programme in 2022 as Covid-19 restrictions eased.

Growing up, Maybelline Ooi's dream was to be a nurse and care for the sick. However, a National University of Singapore (NUS) Overseas Colleges (NOC) internship[55] in Stockholm in 2014 unearthed a new passion in her: to be an entrepreneur.

But that had to wait. Getting her nursing degree was paramount, which she did in 2016. Subsequently, she worked as a nurse to gain practical knowledge and clinical experience.

Then in 2019, she received a fortuitous call from her former lecturer at the Alice Lee Centre for Nursing Studies in NUS. Associate Professor Liaw Sok Ying invited her to tea for a catch-up chat that soon pivoted into a life-changing moment.

Over cake and cups of Earl Grey tea at a café at Orchard Road some months later, Prof Liaw shared that there were companies showing interest in the virtual simulation software she had developed. The program simulates clinical scenarios for trainee nurses to learn in a "real" environment. Ooi was familiar with the software as she was responsible, for ensuring the nurses and their supervisors used it effectively while she was working as Prof Liaw's assistant.

Prof Liaw proposed that Ooi join her as a research assistant to help commercialise the software.

The business potential was apparent to both of them, and she started working for Prof Liaw from August 2020.

Ooi, however, found that she was lacking in one major area: how to create business value and attract investors. Hence, in February 2021, she formed a required team and joined the NUS' Graduate Research Innovation Programme, or GRIP. Over three months, she was hothoused in the ways of entrepreneurship and attained an entrepreneurial badge as she dug deep for pointers in the case studies of successful entrepreneurs.

Post-hothousing, Ooi co-founded VIRTUAI as an NUS GRIP spin-off to commercialise Prof Liaw's clinical scenario simulation software.

VIRTUAI received seed funding from NUS and pitched for funds from external investors. NUS venture managers and GRIP mentors also guided her on how to turn a research project into a business.

The creation of VIRTUAI exemplifies one of the key pillars in NOC's vision of its next stage of growth; that is, to see NOC alumni enter the deep tech sector.

Mapping Out NOC's Future

Having succeeded in creating a pipeline of entrepreneurs, NOC leaders took the next logical step: pair entrepreneurial alumni with NUS researchers and scientists to commercialise the university's discoveries.

There is even a special name for start-ups based on research and engineering innovation. They are labelled "deep tech" and supported by NUS initiatives like GRIP.

The university's plan to develop deep tech start-ups includes extending GRIP to those outside NUS and opening the doors of NOC to students at other Singapore universities as well as those doing their PhD. The aim is to double the annual NOC intake.

The first cohort of non-NUS students will be from the Singapore University of Technology and Design (SUTD). They will start in 2023. No limit has been set on the number to be admitted. They just have to demonstrate that they are entrepreneurial.

This alliance, signed by NUS and SUTD on 14 July 2021, is the first of such collaboration between two Singapore universities. They will work together on entrepreneurship education, research and innovation activities, as well as commercialising research. Both will also share expertise and facilities, according to the Memorandum of Understanding signed by NUS President Tan Eng Chye and SUTD President Chong Tow Chong.

The increase in NOC's annual intake will begin in 2022 until it reaches about 600 by 2025. Previously, the yearly NOC intake was about 300 students. As in the past, no precise quota has been set for each year. **"It depends on the quality of the applicants we get each time,"** said Vice Provost (Technology-Enhanced and Experiential Learning) and NOC Director Professor Chee Yeow Meng.

Part of the bigger pool will comprise PhD students. With about 3,000 PhD students in NUS, Prof Chee is optimistic that around 10 per cent, or 300, can be coaxed to join the programme each year. This would be on top of the 300 or so undergraduates who participate in NOC yearly.

The NOC programme was terribly exciting for Prof Chee Yeow Meng, Vice Provost (Technology-Enhanced) and Experiential Learning) and NOC director, because it is designed to nurture innovation leaders of the future.

NOC had earlier welcomed postgraduate students, but only five Master's students applied. **"We think the programme wasn't attractive because Master's degrees can be a one-year programme. If they do a year's internship overseas under NOC, they will receive their degrees only after two years,"** he pointed out.

With the doctoral students, NOC will adopt a different approach. It will ride on the university's PhD by Innovation programme, which is scheduled to be launched in 2023. These students will pursue their PhDs based on applied research; that is, finding solutions to problems. Traditionally, PhD students do curiosity-based research that leads to new discoveries.

The training will be as rigorous, said Prof Chee.

> Instead of writing a thesis, the doctoral students will solve a problem by developing new systems and, hopefully, business plans. They also must publish their findings in top-tier scientific journals, all of which are peer reviewed, which is important for rigour.

The PhD by Innovation programme[56] is designed to stretch over four years, of which six months will be spent interning overseas with deep tech companies in Silicon Valley in the United States (US), Shenzhen in China, Nagoya in Japan or Tel Aviv in Israel. Such companies develop new products based on scientific discoveries or engineering innovations.

The hoped-for outcome is for students to be fired up by their experience and become technopreneurs, spinning off their applied research into deep tech companies.

The programme's structure will be tweaked for non-PhD students. While on their overseas stint, they will no longer be required to take courses in academic subjects they had enrolled in at their local university. They will do only courses in entrepreneurship and venture creation, said Prof Chee. **"During their internship, I want them to focus solely on entrepreneurship and venture creation."**

Expanding the Global Network

The NOC network comprises more than 15 locations, sited in the US, Canada, Europe and Asia. Pre-pandemic, plans were underway to expand, with centres in Chicago and Boston in the US, Paris in Europe, Chongqing and Guangzhou in China, Nagoya in Japan and Bangkok in Southeast Asia. These cities will offer opportunities for the students to intern in companies specialising in fields such as life sciences, advanced manufacturing and cybersecurity.

By 2021, some of these locations had opened for international travel, prompting Prof Chee to go on the road to finalise arrangements. New contracts were inked with several universities to provide entrepreneurship courses, while at other locations, he searched for entrepreneurs or experts to provide such courses.

On another front, BLOCK71, which has become an icon of Singapore's start-up community, continued to expand. Overseas branches will strengthen the BLOCK71 support system for Singapore start-ups by creating a bigger and stronger global community that would be self-supporting, said Professor Tan Chorh Chuan, NUS President between 2008 and 2017.

In 2015, BLOCK71 San Francisco opened as a co-working space to foster ties between start-up ecosystems in Singapore and the US. Since 2017, BLOCK71 has expanded to Jakarta, Yogyakarta and Bandung in Indonesia, as well as Suzhou in China and Ho Chi Minh City in Vietnam. Plans are afoot to further widen the network.

These facilities were set up with local partners, such as the Salim conglomerate in Indonesia and Vietnamese industrial infrastructure developer Becamex IDC in Ho Chi Minh City.

NUS' role in the tie-ups is to contribute its know-how in creating start-up ecosystems while the local partners are the conduits to the local business community and investors. The two-way flow of talent, technologies and start-ups will not only promote innovation and entrepreneurship but act as a launchpad for each other's start-ups, too, noted Prof Chee.

Another new initiative is NOC's collaboration with NUS to expand its ability to fund start-ups founded by its alumni. This venture fund will be the anchor investor that will provide the critical investment between early stage and Series A.[57]

NOC/NUS will partner BrincArtesian to establish the fund, which is expected to be active in 2023. BrincArtesian is a joint venture between Brinc, an accelerator, and Artesian, an Australian-headquartered asset management firm.

Lightning in a Bottle

When NOC's first cohort flew off to Silicon Valley in 2002, the programme's mission was to groom entrepreneurs in NUS. Many thought it would fail. Today, after many ups and downs, the 20-year-old venture has succeeded in capturing lightning in a bottle.

A survey has found that NOC alumni are almost 10 times more likely than other NUS graduates to become entrepreneurs within six months of graduation. Of start-ups in Singapore that have raised more than US$10 million in external funding, almost five per cent are by companies these alumni had formed.[58]

What is its secret? Ask the alumni or those who have worked with them, and all speak of something transformative that takes place when they go through their overseas internship.

Vinod Nair, founder of financial portal MoneySmart, sums up the perspectives of many alumni.

> 66 When we study other entrepreneurs in the world who are building or have built big start-ups, we realise that there's nothing special about them. They are just like us, regular people who founded start-ups. This gives us the confidence that you don't need to be a rocket scientist or genius to start a company. 99

Dr Jui Lim, CEO of SGInnovate,[59] shares the sentiment: **"The kids were transformed. They acquired bravado and confidence. For those with an entrepreneurial bent and self-declared proclivities, the internship is key."**

Serial entrepreneur-turned-venture capitalist Ong Peng Tsin goes as far as to say that the NOC programme tend to make them ill-suited for more conventional work in traditional multinational companies. **"I talked to many of the NOC students. After they see what's possible overseas, they don't feel comfortable working in traditional companies. So, they launch start-ups."**

Prof Ho Teck Hua, Senior Deputy President and Provost of NUS, believed the NOC programme was crucial for entrepreneurship, giving potential founders a ringside view of failure and success.

NUS Senior Deputy President and Provost Professor Ho Teck Hua believes that the deep immersion in a start-up environment is what transformed the students, "because doing something hands-on makes learning more concrete and much more memorable".

He said: **"They witness and experience first-hand success, failure and recovery. This helps them learn how to be resilient in the face of adversity."**

NOC's subsequent steps in diversifying the types of start-ups available at each location is yet another factor. **"It allows the students to help develop exciting technologies in cities that host leading companies in specified fields; for example, food science in Amsterdam, maritime digital technology in Oslo and retail and e-commerce in Paris."**

Moving forward, the challenge is not just to create more entrepreneurs, but also to leverage on the network that has been created. Professorial Fellow (Entrepreneurship) at NUS, Dr Francis Yeoh, sees tremendous potential in the NOC network of about 3,600 alumni. He cited Y Combinator, an accelerator in the US, as an example. It had developed more than 3,000 global start-ups, including Stripe, Airbnb and Dropbox.

❝ The Y Combinator alumni have enormous value. They have the drive and the connections. As an alumnus, you have access to engineers, investors or mentors to connect to the network and get the support you need," he said. "So, NOC should build a stronger alumni for members to share knowledge and help each other. ❞

Aileen Sim, an NOC alumni who went to Pennsylvania in 2005, agreed. **"Many NOC alumni are my friends, and we support each other. Whenever I've a problem, I call one of them. Or when I need to hire someone with specific skills, I send out a group message. Someone will always respond."**

The alumni invest in NOC start-ups as well, noted Foo Tiang Lim of the NOC 2009 batch. **"Whenever there's an opportunity for investment, we will get the news, and those who want to invest will follow up,"** added Foo, partner and co-founder of venture capital firm, Forge Ventures.

As early as 2010, the NOC programme received the thumbs up from an independent International Advisory Panel.[60] The experts, tasked to review NOC's progress and achievements in its first decade, found it to be an effective educational programme. NUS was also at the forefront of a development wherein universities were increasingly facing demand that they contribute to a "Third Mission", their October 2010 report said. This new mission is entrepreneurship training, research, and outreach activity, on top of the traditional missions of research and teaching.

Big Dreams: NUS, A Start-Up University

The contribution of NOC in growing entrepreneurship in Singapore is indisputable. It laid the foundation for NUS to become a start-up university, where people with a business bent can learn venture creation and entrepreneurship. In doing so, it has broadened the university's role beyond simply training manpower for industry.

In a post-Covid-19 world, NUS President Tan Eng Chye envisioned NUS playing a leading role in Singapore's start-up environment, something akin to Stanford University's position as the anchor for the start-up ecosystem in Silicon Valley.

Writing in the 28 May 2021 issue of *Times Higher Education,*[61] he said, **"The profound challenges confronting us will require fresh thinking and bold solutions."**

Universities, he added, have a unique opportunity to shape the future, by re-envisioning themselves as enablers of innovation that will encourage new businesses and advance societal well-being.

NOC will enable NUS to re-envision itself as enablers of innovation that would encourage new businesses and advance societal well-being, said NUS President Prof Tan Eng Chye.

Prof Freddy Boey, Deputy President (Innovation and Enterprise), hopes to see more NOC alumni set up deep tech start-ups.

The university's Deputy President (Innovation and Enterprise) Professor Freddy Boey hoped there will be more NOC alumni-founded deep tech start-ups, believing that in one to two years' time, they will help NUS contribute tens of start-ups a year in this sector. **"By then, there will be a flood of entrepreneurs. Many will fail but there will be second and third waves of entrepreneurs. We can't lose this game. My biggest work is to ensure that people trained in NUS will be entrepreneurial."**

He cited Switzerland as an example of a small country punching above its weight in the start-up world. Its companies are powerhouses in advanced technology especially in food sciences and precision engineering. **"There are big Swiss multinational companies around the world. That's what Singapore needs to have, by growing its own start-ups into giants."**

NUS aims **"to be the university of choice for any young person who wants to get the skills to be an entrepreneur"**, Prof Boey added.

Even as NOC celebrates its success, Prof Shih Choon Fong sounded a warning. The past success is no guarantee of future success, he said. Prof Shih was the guest of honour at the gala dinner held in October 2022 to celebrate NOC's 20th anniversary and BLOCK71's 10th anniversary.

In his speech titled "Do we win the future again, or lose it?", he pointed to the dual challenges of climate change and social inequity which are all crises of the collective and the social.

He called on the NOC/NUS students to harness their entrepreneurial passions to focus on inclusive growth in order to serve people, solve collective problems and share the benefits with society.[62]

The point is reinforced, with figures, by NUS President Prof Tan. **"NOC was the seed for the start-up community in Singapore. Today, NOC companies make up five per cent of Singapore's tech-based start-ups. Over the last 20 years, NOC students and alumni have created more than 1,000 start-ups and, collectively, NOC-founded start-ups have raised more than US$2.5 billion in funding."**

At least two, PatSnap and Carousell, are valued at above US$1 billion.

Reflecting on NOC's 20-year journey, he said that it has allowed NUS to build a solid, vibrant foundation with global nodes and connections.

For the next 20 years, NOC's role would be to expand and deepen its roots in innovation and entrepreneurship. **"Ultimately, this is our vision: Beyond being the top university in Asia, we aim to become the start-up university of the world,"** said Prof Tan.

ENDNOTES

1   Michael Yap, Deputy CEO and Executive Director of Media Development Authority, 2006–2013; Dr Lily Chan, CEO, NUS Enterprise 2006–2019; and Yvonne Kwek, CEO of Innov8, Singtel's corporate venture arm, 2010–2012.

2   PatSnap is an innovation intelligence platform that provides intellectual property and research and development intelligence.

3   Wong, P. K., Ho, Y. P., & Ng, S. J. C. (2019, July). *Nurturing Entrepreneurial Talent: The NUS Overseas Colleges Program. Findings from the inaugural survey of NOC alumni.* NUS Entrepreneurship Centre. https://enterprise.nus.edu.sg/wp-content/uploads/2020/07/Nuturing-Entrepreneurial-Talent-The-NOC-Program-Alumni-Survey-Report-July-2019-Published-report.pdf.

4   In 2002, Venture Manufacturing was renamed Venture Corporation.

5   The National Computer Board was set up in 1981 to drive computerisation in Singapore and to develop the tech industry.

6   Kent Ridge Digital Lab (KRDL) was formed in 1998 as a result of the merger between the Information Technology Institute of the National Computer Board and the R&D Group of the Institute of Systems Science of NUS. KRDL was later merged with the Centre of Singapore Processing to form Laboratories for Information Technology (LIT). Subsequently, LIT was merged with other organisations to form Institute for Infocomm Research.

7   Shih, C.F. (2000). NUS: A Global Knowledge Enterprise: Inaugural address by the Vice Chancellor of the National University of Singapore, Professor Shih Choon Fong on 1 June. Singapore: National University of Singapore.

8   Institute of Materials Research and Engineering (IMRE) was set up in 1997. It is a research institute of the Science and Engineering Research Council (SERC), Agency for Science, Technology and Research (A*STAR).

9   The Association of Southeast Asian Nations (ASEAN) was born in August 1967. It is a political and economic union of 10 countries in Southeast Asia,. It comprises Brunei, Cambodia, Indonesia, Laos, Malaysia, Myanmar, the Philippines, Singapore, Thailand and Vietnam. ASEAN promotes intergovernmental cooperation and facilitates economic, political, military, educational and socio-cultural integration between its members and countries in the Asia-Pacific. Its primary objective was to accelerate economic growth and through that social progress and cultural development.

10 Dr Tony Tan joined the People's Action Party and became Member of Parliament for Sembawang Single Member Constituency (SMC) in 1979. He served in various ministerial portfolios including education, finance and defence. He was appointed Deputy Prime Minister from 1995 to 2005. Dr Tan resigned from the cabinet in 2005 and assumed various chairmanship appointments in the Government of Singapore Investment Corporation. He resigned from his positions in 2010 and successfully contested in the 2011 presidential election as an independent. He was President of Singapore from 2011–2017.

11 Tan, Tony, T.K. (1998). Education in a Globalised Economy. Speech by Dr Tony Tan Keng Yam, Deputy Prime Minister and Minister for Defence at the NTU Ministerial Forum, on 19 February. Singapore: Nanyang Technological University. [Online] Available at: https://www.nas.gov.sg/archivesonline/data/pdfdoc/19980219_0001.pdf.

12 Shih, C.F. 2008. *Shih Choon Fong 2000–2008*. (National University of Singapore). [Online] Available at: https://www.nus.edu.sg/docs/default-source/corporate-files/about/community/vicechancellors/shih-choon-fong.pdf.

13 Stanford University played a central role in the development of Silicon Valley in the southern San Francisco Bay Area into a leading global centre for tech start-ups and companies. Stanford engineering and computer science students were encouraged to found tech companies while many lecturers invested in the young start-ups. Trickha, R. 2015. The Interdependency of Stanford and Silicon Valley. (TechCrunch). [Online]. Available at: https://techcrunch.com/2015/09/04/what-will-stanford-be-without-silicon-valley/.

14 Interviews conducted with Prof Shih Choon Fong over WeChat, Zoom and email between October 2020 and February 2022.

15 NUS Enterprise, the entrepreneurial arm of NUS, plays a pivotal role in advancing innovation and entrepreneurship at NUS and beyond. It was set up in 2001.

16 Prof Wong won the World Entrepreneurship Forum's (WEF) 2015 Entrepreneur for the World Award in the educator category in recognition of his efforts in nurturing entrepreneurs and spreading an entrepreneurial culture in Singapore. Cheok, J. 2018. *NUS Prof Wong Poh Kam wins world entrepreneurship award.* (The Business Times). [Online]. Available at: https://www.businesstimes.com.sg/government-economy/nus-prof-wong-poh-kam-wins-world-entrepreneurship-award.

17 Interviews with Prof Teo Chee Leong between June 2020 and 14 July 2021 in a face-to-face meeting and over email.

18 Adjunct Professor Dr. Casey Chan was Director, Industry and Technology Relations Office, NUS.

19 National University of Singapore. 2002. *Enterprising Education, Educating Enterprise, National University of Singapore Annual Report 2002.* [Online]. Available at: https://www.nus.edu.sg/docs/default-source/annual-report/nus-annualreport-2002.pdf.

20 From interviews with Prof Teo: For receiving the US$5 million grant, the deliverables include the following: Participation in network of top entrepreneurship development centres. Participation will take the form of two-way exchange programmes for faculty and students and collaborative research with top institutes in entrepreneurship development.

Additional course development/educational programmes to build local capabilities. NUS should undertake to develop undergraduate, graduate and executive courses on technopreneurship-related subjects.

Creation of strong Singapore-wide iconic events. Such events could take the form of seminars/forums, symposiums/conferences and competitions, and would involve start-up companies, venture capitalists, as well as executives from top companies looking for promising technologies.

21 The National Science and Technology Board (NSTB) was formed in 1991 to formulate and implement long-term research and development strategies for Singapore. Its aim was to transform Singapore into an innovation-driven economy in which industry-driven research and development would help the country become more competitive internationally. It funded different organisations to do this. In 2005, it was renamed as A*STAR.

22 Interviews with Prof Teo Chee Leong between June 2020 and 14 July 2021.

23 Interviews with Prof Teo Chee Leong between June 2020 and 14 July 2021.

24 Interview with Mrs Tok Yu Ling in July 2020.

25 PSA Corporation was set up in 1964 to operate the Singapore port. It also expanded its business oveseas. In December 2003, PSA International became the holding company for the PSA Group of companies.

26 Tay, K.F. 2013. NOC Alumni remembers Professor Jacob Phang. e27. [Online] Available at: https://e27.co/noc-alumni-remembers-professor-jacob-phang/.

27 Bio*One Capital is a subsidiary of EDB Investments, focused on investing in the biomedical sciences industry. EDB Investments is the corporate investment arm of the Economic Development Board tasked with developing strategies that enhance Singapore's position as a global centre for business, innovation, and talent.

28 SPRING Singapore was merged with International Enterprise Singapore to form Enterprise Singapore to help Singapore businesses grow and internalise. The start-up function that was in SPRING Singapore moved to the new organisation. Yahya, Y. 2017. IE Singapore, Spring Singapore to merge to better help local firms go global. (The Straits Times). [Online] Available at: https://www.straitstimes.com/business/economy/ie-singapore-spring-singapore-to-merge-to-better-help-local-firms-go-global.

29 Interviews with Dr Lily Chan between August and October 2021.

30 Startup Genome. 2019. Global Startup Ecosystem Report 2019. [Online]. Available at: https://startupgenome.com/reports/global-startup-ecosystem-report-2019.

31 Wikipedia. 2022. Media Development Authority. [Online] Available at: https://en.wikipedia.org/wiki/Media_Development_Authority [Accessed 16 August 2022]. Media Development Authority. 2012. World Class Media Cluster. Interactive Digital Media. [Online] Available at: https://www.imda.gov.sg/-/media/imda/files/about/resources/corporate-publications/mda-html/2012/chapter1-7.htm [Accessed 16 August 2022].

32 Interview with Hugh Mason and Wong Meng Weng held between June and September 2021.

33 Interview with Prof Tan Chorh Chuan in August 2021.

34 Chng, G. 2015. 'Search on for more start up 'launch pads' (The Straits Times). [Online] Available at: https://www.straitstimes.com/business/search-on-for-more-start-up-launch-pads [Accessed 16 August 2022].

35 NUS Enterprise. 2007. *PatSnap*. [Online] Available at: https://enterprise.nus.edu.sg/startup-story/patsnap/ [Accessed 16 August 2022].

36 Options: The Edge Malaysia. 2019. *Sabah-born PatSnap CEO Jeffrey Tiong on creating the world's leading R&D analytics software*. [Online] Available at: https://www.optionstheedge.com/topic/people/sabah-born-patsnap-ceo-jeffrey-tiong-creating-world%E2%80%99s-leading-rd-analytics-software [Accessed 16 August 2022].

37 Lai. L. 2018. *PatSnap CEO Jeffrey Tiong named EY Entrepreneur of the Year 2018* (The Business Times). [Online] Available at: https://www.businesstimes.com.sg/companies-markets/patsnap-ceo-jeffrey-tiong-named-ey-entrepreneur-of-the-year-2018 [Accessed 16 August 2022].

38 The Software Report. 2020. *The Top 50 SaaS CEOs of 2020*. [Online] Available at: https://www.thesoftwarereport.com/the-top-50-saas-ceos-of-2020/ [Accessed 16 August 2022].

39 Forbes 30 Under 30 Asia. 2016. *Enterprise Technology*. [Online] Available at: https://www.forbes.com/30-under-30-asia-2016/enterprise-tech/#b2ef90578fe3 [Accessed 16 August 2022].

40 NUS Computing. 2019. *NUS Computing alumna receives NUS Outstanding Young Alumni Award*. [Online] Available at: https://www.comp.nus.edu.sg/news/archives/y2019/2019-nus-alumni-awards/ [Accessed 16 August 2022].

41 Shopee was launched in November 2015 by Sea, the largest public-listed company in Southeast Asia. Today, the Singapore-based company has expanded into about 16 markets around the world and has offices in more than 20 cities. It ranks first on Best APAC Buzz Rankings 2020 put out by YouGov, a British market research and data analytics firm, and at No. 8 in YouGov's Best Global Brands 2020.

42 Shopee is the leading Southeast Asian e-commerce platform with the most visits. Like other e-commerce outlets it has been struggling in an increasingly uncertain global economic outlook. Shopee's parent company has cut back it's full-year e-commerce revenue outlook in May 2022 to US$8.5 billion, down from US$8.9 billion. Sea did not provide e-commerce forecast for the future. In September 2019, it opened its regional headquarters in a new, six-storey building in Kent Ridge that spans 244,000 sq. ft. The space is nearly six times larger than its previous office and can house up to 3,000 employees, according to a CNA news report on 3 September 2019, headlined "Shopee opens new regional HQ in Singapore as it rides growth in Southeast Asia".

43 The interview with Chris Feng was done in August 2021. A graduate in computer science (Honours, First Class) from the National University of Singapore, he had worked in other companies before joining Sea in early 2014. They include European venture capital company Rocket Internet SE where he was Managing Director from January 2012 to February 2014 and was involved in establishing online ventures such as Lazada and Zalora. Lazada is an international e-commerce company backed by Rocket and owned by the Alibaba group, while Zalora is a leading online fashion, beauty and lifestyle platform. Feng went on the NOC programme in 2003. He did his 12-month internship at TuVox in Cupertino, a city in California. Founded in 2001, TuVox was a major player in speech recognition technology and was acquired in July 2010 by West Interactive, a leading provider of automated customer contact solutions.

44 Asia's ecommerce market will grow by 22.4 per cent to US$1.7 trillion in 2020 and reach US$2.45 trillion by 2024, predicts Statista, a German company that specialises in market and consumer data.

45 i.JAM is the Interactive Digital Media Jumpstart and Mentor initiative. A micro-funding scheme, it is a key component of the Interactive Digital Media Programme Office (IDMPO) set up to develop Singapore into a vibrant media hub. i.JAM seeds young start-ups or individuals with exciting research and development ideas with a grant of up to S$50,000 to prove their ideas and get a chance to be entrepreneurs in the high growth IDM space. Available at: https://www.imda.gov.sg/content-and-news/press-releases-and-speeches/archived/mda/press-releases/2007/mda-administers-new-microfunding-scheme-to-stimulate-bottomup-innovation-in-idm [Accessed 16 August 2022].

46 Rahman, N.A. Mukunthan, M. 2016. Syed Omar Ali Aljunied. [Online] Singapore Infopedia. Available at: https://eresources.nlb.gov.sg/infopedia/articles/SIP_847_2004-12-29.html [Accessed 16 August 2022].

47 e27 was originally founded in 2007 as a start-up blog.

48 Shop.org is a division of the National Retail Federation, United States. It holds annual conferences for the retail industry over the phone in Singapore.

49 SPRING Singapore was merged with another government agency International Enterprise Singapore, to form Enterprise Singapore to champion enterprise growth. [See note 28].

50 Wong, P. K., Ho, Y. P., & Ng, S. J. C. 2019. *Nurturing Entrepreneurial Talent: The NUS Overseas Colleges Programme: Findings from the inaugural survey of NOC alumni. NUS Enterprise. July 2019.* [Online] Available at: https://enterprise.nus.edu.sg/wp-content/uploads/2020/07/Nuturing-Entrepreneurial-Talent-The-NOC-Program-Alumni-Survey-Report-July-2019-Published-report.pdf [Accessed?].

51 The HYSTA 2007 Conference was held in Santa Clara Convention Centre in California. It was called China, Globalisation and the Shifting Global Power Equation. Former US Vice-President Al Gore was one of the speakers. The conference was organised by the Hua Yuan Science and Technology Association, a non-profit organisation to exchange business ideas, promote cultural exchange and foster ties between Chinese entrepreneurs and executives in Silicon Valley.

52 Mai Nguyen was interviewed in Vietnam via Zoom in January and February 2021.

53 FabAcademy Taipei opened in May 2013 and is managed by Taiwan Makers Association. It is a non-profit association for makers who want to learn and use digital fabrication tools.

54 SARS. (n.d.). Retrieved September 2, 2022, from Wikipedia: https://en.wikipedia.org/wiki/SARS.

55 Three interviews over Zoom, phone and email were conducted with Maybelline Ooi in September 2021. Ooi interned with Swedish Care International in Stockholm between August 2014 and July 2015.

56 The NUS PhD by Innovation four-year programme is aimed at entrepreneurial scientists who want to turn their research into commercial products. Part of the programme requires candidates to complete a six-month NOC overseas internship in major start-up hubs including Silicon Valley, US and Tel Aviv, Israel.

57 Series A refers to the part of a start-up's journey after it has proven its business case, launched its operations and is bringing in revenue.

58 Ministry of Education. 2021. "NUS Graduate Employment Survey 2012-2021." [Online] Available at *https://www.moe.gov.sg/-/media/files/post-secondary/ges-2021/web-publication-nus-ges-2021.pdf* [Accessed 2 September 2022]; NUS Overseas Colleges. 2022. "NOC Alumni Survey 2021/22."

59 SGInnovate is a private organisation owned by the Singapore government which helps entrepreneurial scientists build deep tech start-ups.

60 The International Advisory Panel helps NUS Enterprise to evaluate the NOC programme, review its progress, assess its outcomes and achievements, and consider its long-term goals and priorities. The IAP, set up in 2010, comprised Prof Jerome Engel (Chairman), Adjunct Professor, Haas School of Business, University of California, Berkeley; Dr Orna Berry, chief scientist of Israel between 1997 and 2019; and Prof Erkko Autio, Professor in Technology Transfer and Entrepreneurship, Imperial College Business School, London. They were selected based on their relevant expertise in the various areas of entrepreneurship and collectively cover a diverse range of expertise on entrepreneurship education.

61 *Times Higher Education* provides data, insight and expertise on higher education worldwide.

62 The full text of Prof Shih Choon Fong's speech "Do we win the future again, or lose it" can be found in Annex 1. The NOC 20th anniversary and BLOCK71's 10th anniversary gala dinner was held on 26 October 2022 at the Shangri-la Hotel.

List of Common Acronyms

ASEAN	Association of Southeast Asian Nations
BLOCK71	The initiative/programme by NUS Enterprise which started off at Block 71 Ayer Rajah Crescent
Blk71	Block 71 Ayer Rajah Crescent (physical location)
NUS	National University of Singapore
i.JAM	Interactive Digital Media Jumpstart and Mentor initiative
MDA	Media Development Authority
NEC	NUS Entrepreneurship Centre
NOC	NUS Overseas Colleges
BHAG	Big Hairy Audacious Goal
JTC	Jurong Town Corporation
ACE	Action Community for Entrepreneurship
SARS	Severe Acute Respiratory Syndrome
HDB	Housing and Development Board

Acknowledgements

NUS Overseas Colleges would like to extend their thanks to their supporters and to all who have helped in their journey. Below is a non-exhaustive list of names:

NUS

Prof Tan Eng Chye
Prof Ho Teck Hua
Prof Freddy Boey
Prof Chee Yeow Meng
Dr Francis Yeoh
Prof Lim Pin
Prof Tan Chorh Chuan

NOC FOUNDERS

Prof Shih Choon Fong
Prof Jacob Pang
Prof Teo Chee Leong
Dr Lily Chan
Prof Wong Poh Kam

NOC ALLIES AND CHAMPIONS

Png Cheong Boon
Edwin Chow
Dr Jui Lim
Michael Yap
Tom Kosnik
Yvonne Kwek
Tan Ying Lan

Wong Meng Weng
Hugh Mason
Ong Peng Tsin
Inderjit Singh
Chandra Bodapati
Per Bjorkland
Christian Heckemann

NOC ALUMNI

Bjorn Lee
Justin Lee
Darius Cheung
Mohan Belani
Audrey Tan
Goh Yiping
Gwendolyn Regina Tan
Charmain Tan
Quek Siu Rui
Kelly Choo
Jeffrey Tiong
Dixon Chan
Rex Huang
Guan Dian
Vinod Nair
Hew Joon Yeng
Grace Chia

Chris Feng Zhimin

Tay Yan Bing Crispina

Sivamani Varun

Sriram Krishnan

Chua Pei Fen

Mahesh Kumar

Charmain Tan

Nguyen Thi Thanh Mai

Brenda Toh Yi Ling

Chean Yujun

Syed Ahmad bin Abdullah Aljunied

Syed Ali bin Abdullah Aljunied

Syed Muhammed bin Abdullah Aljunied

Jacky Yap

Gordon Ng

Varun Chatterjee

Linawaty Maria

Tay Kae Fong

Teo Jason Kian Jin

Yak Chin Wee

Pratyay Jaidev

Gary Teo

Esabel Lee

Denise Yeo

Andrew Sim

Alvin Ryanputra

Pradeep Paulroopson

Cordillia Ann Tan Mei Yu

Zhi Cheng

Ryan Chong

Vincent Woon

Shreyan Singh

Maybelline Ooi

Augustine Chia

EDITORIAL TEAM

Siva Arasu (Book Editor)

Irene Hoe

Melody Zaccheus

Natasha Zachariah

NUS ENTERPRISE

Cheng Tai Chin

Mrs Tok Yu Ling

Hui Kwok Leong

Brian Koh

Gang Chern Sun

Harpreet Singh

Xander Khoo

Ho Geer How

Benedict Lim

ANNEX

Do We Win the Future Again, or Lose It?

Shih Choon Fong
University Professor, National University of Singapore, Singapore

This chapter is reproduced from a speech delivered by Prof Shih Choon Fong at the NUS Gala Dinner, NOC 20th Anniversary and BLOCK71 10th Anniversary, 26 October 2022, Shangri-La Hotel, Singapore.

NUS President Tan Eng Chye
Distinguished Guests, Partners, Alumni, Friends, Colleagues and well-wishers of NOC and BLOCK71

This evening's Gala dinner has significance for many here, myself included. It was 20 years and 10 months ago when NUS dreamers and adventurers landed in Silicon Valley. It was the beginning of a bold experiment to ignite the entrepreneurial spirit at NUS, and we started with the young. Right after National Day this year, Channel News Asia screened a special programme called "Startup University." It paid this tribute to all of us who have labored at NUS:

I quote:

" NUS has emerged as the most influential force in Singapore's start-up ecosystem. NUS Enterprise, the University's entrepreneurial arm, has been playing a pivotal role in advancing innovation and entrepreneurship. **"**

Well done NUS. Well done NOC. Well done BLOCK71.

Today, NOC has more than 3,600 alumni, with over 15 entrepreneurial hubs established across the globe. Nine NUS-supported startups have become unicorns and our alumni have founded more than 1,000 startups. Our students, including the first 14 adventurous souls who went to Silicon Valley in 2002, deserve our admiration. Please give a hand to them.

In this celebratory moment, I also want to acknowledge that these dreamers and adventurers at NUS have been well supported by key academics. First and foremost was the late Jacob Phang. A Cambridge-trained engineer, Jacob was no ordinary professor, but a man willing to take risks. As kindred spirits, we both wanted our students to experience the crucible of entrepreneurship, knowing it could not be taught in the classroom. Jacob passed away too soon, and we all owe him a debt of gratitude.

If Jacob, as Founding CEO and pilot of Enterprise, was Captain James Kirk, then Lily Chan, the second CEO was Captain Picard. Both were supported by Teo Chee Leong, Founding Director of NOC and Wong Poh Kam, Founding Director of NUS Entrepreneurship Centre. They flew Starship Enterprise high and far.

But it was our dreamer-adventurers — the NOC interns and alumni — who went where few Singaporeans had gone before. It is because of them we are having this dinner tonight.

As we gather to celebrate, what are we to learn from our success?

When NOC started 20 years ago, Singapore had just come through the Asian Financial Crisis, SARS and the Bali bombing, and the world had experienced 9/11. Today, just barely out of the pandemic crisis, we find ourselves threatened by geopolitical fissures, facing ominous ecological crisis and pressures from economic inequalities.

I put before you that if the future has to be won, it has to be won differently. We must adapt what has worked well for what is now a very changed landscape. Globalisation, growth, technology and more are being questioned and challenged as never before. Let me therefore shed light by asking you to remember the nature of our journey at NUS.

THE FIRST PHASE OF THE NUS JOURNEY

The first phase of the NUS journey was the post-independence years, when Singapore was wooing MNCs to spur industrialisation, and the university's purpose was to churn out competent graduates who would get their jobs done. But then, as I said earlier, Singapore at the turn of the millennium experienced several shocks and had to restructure its economy and become a "Knowledge-based Economy".

When I took up the role of NUS Vice Chancellor, I knew that NUS had to change. Primarily, the students' mindset and thinking process needed to be sharpened through real-life encounters. Singapore's pressure cooker examination culture was not enough. They would need a new kind of pressure that came from complexity, not conformity; from difference, not sameness; and from encountering people who dreamt their own dreams and pursued them with astonishing vigour and energy.

In my inaugural address on 1 June 2000, I articulated a vision: NUS will be to Singapore what Stanford is to Silicon Valley, a knowledge enterprise transcending boundaries. NUS Enterprise, as our vehicle, would enable NUS to learn and spar with the best, to innovate and be freed from traditional rules, to be flexible and respond faster. NUS Enterprise would push the boundaries of best entrepreneurial practices and launch major innovations.[1]

The first initiative was the NUS Overseas Colleges (NOC), and we would travel to Silicon Valley.

Launching NOC in Silicon Valley was like building, retrofitting and piloting a first-of-its-kind plane while in mid-air. The runway was bumpy and there was turbulence and headwinds all the way. But there was no turning back. With Jacob as pilot, assisted by co-pilot Chee Leong, 14 interns landed in Silicon Valley in 2002. That was the defining moment. Till then, our NUS dreamers were accustomed to life in an orderly city-state where things ran predictably and smoothly. Now they were thrust into an entrepreneurial hotspot where untidiness seeded germs of creativity. In this different world our student trailblazers proved their mettle. Many more followed. The rest is history.

THE SECOND PHASE OF THE NUS JOURNEY

All successful ventures will have their naysayers. Naysayers serve a purpose. They give reasons why the venture is ill-conceived, and not work. In the language of flight engineering, naysayers represent gravity and headwinds. Invariably, they sharpen our thinking and resolve, forcing us to reassess our choices: to pursue takeoff or stay with the status quo. I therefore mean it sincerely when I say that all of us have played our roles well and contributed to the success of NOC.

---

1   Shih, C.F. (2000). NUS: A Global Knowledge Enterprise: Inaugural Address by the Vice Chancellor of the National University of Singapore, Professor Shih Choon Fong on 1 June. Singapore: National University of Singapore.

However, I would be remiss if tonight, I only celebrated with you without a serious talk about the new challenges brought by a changing world.

In Phase 1, our university needed to churn out technical personnel for the MNC production lines. But when they left for cheaper places, our strategy was no longer fit for its purpose. In Phase 2, we repurposed ourselves for a knowledge-based economy, unleashing the energies for knowledge, creativity and entrepreneurship.

As successful as Phase 2 has been, economic success has resulted in unintended pain for quite a few. Any of our current students in Silicon Valley and San Francisco can attest to the homeless tent-cities sprouting under the highways, not just in the Bay Area, but in other parts of the United States. The Silicon Valley Success Story, which inspired so many, has had its unintended consequences. While Singapore doesn't have tent-cities, nevertheless the dynamics inherent in the Bay Area are everywhere else present, including here in Singapore: extraordinary success for the few, coupled with enlarging pockets of distress for far too many.

In the past years, some in Singapore have spoken of our pear-shaped income distribution with the top doing well and the bottom suffering. Globally, climate change has a greater negative effect on those at the lower end of the pear — the less-developed countries, and especially people who are already living precarious lives. We must ask: Are our attitudes, goals and strategies fit for purpose in this new landscape?

THE THIRD PHASE OF THE NUS JOURNEY

An I-oriented entrepreneurial spirit was right for the challenges we had faced 20 years back. But I-orientation, and all that is implied by way of economic growth, governance, motivation, leadership and responsibility, is no longer sufficient and is even a problem. Today's dual challenges of climate change and social inequity are all crises of the collective and the social. The world now needs business leaders and entrepreneurs who have a we-orientation. We need inclusive growth. We-orientation is now required of leaders and citizens, and they must urgently harness the entrepreneurial passions of I-orientation to serve people, solve collective problems and share the benefits.[2]

Today, we are compelled to face the new realities. Our mental orientation must now change to encompass greater complexity, our hearts must enlarge to include others, and our strategies, educational policies and actions must follow suit.

While the future cannot be seen, the choices we make now will shape our future. With a changing local, regional and global landscape, we need a new generation of leaders, and especially of the young, to bring about change and make us fit for purpose for a world in which all can thrive in. There will be naysayers, but as I have said, the purpose of gravity and headwind is to enable you to build something that will take-off and fly high and far.

---

2   Shih, C. F. (2022, October 20). *Reflections on 20 years of NOC: Part 3 – Re-envisioning entrepreneurship.* Retrieved from NUSnews: https://news.nus.edu.sg/reflections-on-20-years-of-noc-part-3--re-envisioning-entrepreneurship/

On this note, I now invite you to envision with me an NUS in 2042.

There is a special report by the United Nations noting the contribution of several generations of "we-oriented" entrepreneurs coming out of NUS. Its cover page reads: "Singapore and Southeast Asia achieve inclusive growth and happiness … NUS entrepreneurs led the way".

I recall an Indonesian saying that goes like this:

"My past belongs to me. Your past belongs to you. But the future belongs to us."

I wish each of you the very very best in your continuing journey of life.

NOC
PHOTO
GALLERY

Members of the NOC International Advisory Panel 2010. From left: Prof Jerome S. Engel, Faculty Director of UC Berkeley Haas Centre for Entrepreneurship and Chairman of the Advisory Panel and two other members, Dr Orna Berry (second from left) and Prof Erkko Autio, (third from left); and Professor Teo Chee Leong, NOC Director (right).

2001 Dinner with NOC champions: Prof Tom Kosnik (left), a consulting professor at Stanford Technology Ventures Program, San Francisco; Prof Wong Poh Kam (centre), Founding Director of NUS Entrepreneurship Centre and NOC academic advisor; and Dr Lena Ramfelt, (right) who taught entrepreneurship at the KTH Royal Institute of Technology, Stockholm.

*Wong Meng Weng,
co-founder of
Joyful Frog Digital
Innovation (JFDI),
a familiar figure in
Blk71, and his frog
mascot.*

*Pratyay Jaidev (second from right) with colleagues from Erium GMBH in
Munich. He arrived in February 2020 and was recalled home the following
month due to the Covid-19 pandemic.*

NUS-Kungliga Tekniska Hogskolan (KTH) leaders posing for a photo after inking the NOC partnership. Dr Tony Tan (fourth from left), who was travelling in Scandinavia at that time, attended the event.
Also present were Prof Anders Flodström, then Rector of KTH (third from left),
Prof Shih Choon Fong, then NUS President (fifth from left); Prof Jacob Phang (right).

Prof Wong Poh Kam, NOC's academic advisor (second row, fourth from right, wearing a coat), visited Google in 2008 with the first batch of NOC Singapore students.

NOC alumni Shaik Jifridin and Cordillia Tan (seated right) sharing with NOC Director Prof Chee Yeow Meng (seated left) in Singapore on lessons learnt during their internship.

*tenCube led by co-founder Darius Cheung won the Start-up
@ Singapore business competition in 2006.*

*Gwendolyn Regina
Tan (fourth from left)
who went to Silicon
Valley in 2005 attended
a gathering with her
fellow NOC batch mates.*

Prime Minister Lee Hsien Loong opened LaunchPad @ one-north in January 2015 and toured an exhibition showcasing the developments there, including BLOCK71 activities.

NOC 20TH ANNIVERSARY GALA DINNER AT THE SHANGRI-LA HOTEL, 2022

The pioneers of NOC who overcame the many challenges to develop a world leading entrepreneurship training programme for NUS. From left: Tom Kosnik, former Consulting Professor for NOC; Prof Teo Chee Leong, former Director of NOC; Dr Lily Chan, former CEO of NUS Enterprise; Mrs Jacob Phang, wife of the late NOC co-founder, Prof Jacob Phang; Prof Shih Choon Fong, former NUS President and co-founder of NOC; Prof Wong Poh Kam, former Senior Director of Entrepreneurship Centre, NUS; Prof Tan Eng Chye, NUS President.

Prof Shih Choon Fong (fourth from left) cutting the big birthday cake to celebrate the birthdays of NOC and BLOCK71. Standing with him were (from left) Prof Tan Eng Chye; Dr Lily Chan; Mrs Jacob Phang (extreme right).

Time capsule launched containing memorabilia such as Prof Shih Choon Fong's favourite salmon tie, past designs of NOC T-shirts and other information on history of NOC and BLOCK71. Witnessing the event were: (from left), Prof Chee Yeow Meng; Prof Tan Eng Chye,; Dr Lily Chan; Prof Shih Choon Fong; Dr Tan Chin Nam, former Permanent Secretary, Ministry of Information, Communications and the Arts; Mrs Jacob Phang; Edgar Hardless, CEO, Singtel Innov8; Prof Freddy Boey, NUS Deputy President, Innovation & Enterprise; and Yvonne Kwek, former CEO of Singtel Innov8.

Prof Chee Yeow Meng, Vice-Provost of Technology-Enhanced and Experiential Learning and Director of NOC, was the host for NOC and BLOCK71's birthday bash at the NOC 20th anniversary gala dinner.

Prof Shih Choon Fong introduced the NOC programme in 2001 when he was NUS President (2000–2008). He was the guest-of-honour at the gala dinner. Seated next to him (first from right) is the current NUS President, Prof Tan Eng Chye.

Dr Lily Chan, the second CEO of NUS Enterprise, highlighted the persistence and determination of NOC alumni in building their start-ups.

For the time capsule launched at the NOC's 20th anniversary gala dinner, Yvonne Kwek added two photos of BLOCK71 taken in 2011 and 2017. They capture the development of the building in One North. Kwek as the CEO of Innov8, the venture arm of Singtel, played a pioneering role in the development of BLOCK71.

Prof Tan Eng Chye (second from left); Prof Shih Choon Fong (third from left); and Assoc Prof Teo Chee Leong (extreme right) striking a happy pose with Carousell co-founders Quek Siu Rui (extreme left), Marcus Tan (fourth from left) and Lucas Ngoo (fifth from left).

It was time to renew friendships when about 480 NOC alumni and guests came together to celebrate NOC's 20th birthday party held on 26 October 2022 at the Shangri-la Hotel. The party also celebrated the 10th anniversary of BLOCK71 which started in 2011.